HOLT
2
FRENCH

Allez, viens!®

Activities for Communication

HOLT, RINEHART AND WINSTON

A Harcourt Classroom Education Company

Austin · New York · Orlando · Atlanta · San Francisco · Boston · Dallas · Toronto · London

Contributing Writers

Communicative Activities	Paul Cowap Austin, TX
	Jamie Jones James Bowie High School Austin, TX
	Janet Grady Lumley Corpus Christi, TX
	Margaret Sellstrom Austin, TX
Realia	Betty Peltier Batz-sur-Mer, France
	Anne Nerenz Eastern Michigan University Ypsilanti, MI
Situation Cards	Barbara Kelley Parkway Central High School Chesterfield, MO

Cover Photo Credits
Group of students: Marty Granger/HRW Photo; Quebec sign: Marty Granger/HRW Photo
CD: Digital imagery® © 2003 Photodisc, Inc.

Art Credits
All art, unless otherwise noted, by Holt, Rinehart and Winston.

Photography Credits
Page 17 (all); 18 (all), HRW Photo/Sam Dudgeon; 75 (all), HRW Photo/Marty Granger/Edge Productions; 92 (all), HRW Photo/Sam Dudgeon; 115, Maladie d'Amour. Sidney et Bom © 1988 by Editions du Lombard, Bruxelles-Paris; 125(cl), © Sony Records, 125 (cr), © Virgin Records; 125 (bl), Sony Records; 127 (cl), Meurtres à 30 000 km/s, de Christophe Lambert © 1998 Hachette Jeunesse; 127 (bl), Déchets, la planète en péril, de Sylvia Vaisman, © 1998 Casterman éditeurs; 127 (br), Max, mon frère, de Sigrid Zeevaert © 1998 Bayard Poche

ALLEZ, VIENS! is a trademark licensed to Holt, Rinehart and Winston, registered in the United States of America and/or other jurisdictions.

Printed in the United States of America

ISBN 0-03-065563-3

2 3 4 5 6 7 066 05 04 03 02

Contents

SITUATION CARDS

To the Teacher

Oral communication is the most challenging language skill to develop and test. The *Allez, viens!* *Activities for Communication* book helps students to develop their speaking skills and gives them opportunities to communicate in a variety of situations. The Communicative Activities and Situation Cards provide a variety of information-gap activities, interviews, and role-plays to assist students with the progression from closed-ended practice to more creative, open-ended use of French. The authentic documents in the Realia section provide students with additional reading practice using material written by and for native speakers. Included with the Realia are teaching suggestions and student activities showing how to integrate the four skills and culture into your realia lesson. With the focus on conversation and real-life context, the activities in this book will help your students achieve the goal of genuine interaction.

Each chapter of *Activities for Communication* provides:

- **Communicative Activities**   In each of the twelve chapters, three communicative, pair-work activities encourage students to use French in realistic conversation, in settings where they must seek and share information. The activities provide cooperative language practice and encourage students to take risks with language in a relaxed, uninhibiting, and non-threatening setting. The activities which correspond to each **étape** provide students with opportunities to practice using the functions, vocabulary, and grammar presented in that chapter section. Each activity may be used upon completion of the **étape** as a Performance Assessment, or may be recorded on audio or video tape for inclusion in students' portfolios. The activities may also be used as an informal review of the **étape** to provide additional oral practice.

- **Realia**   In each chapter there are three reproducible pieces of realia that relate to the chapter theme and reflect life and culture in French-speaking countries. Finding they can read and understand documents intended for native speakers gives students a feeling of accomplishment that encourages them to continue learning. Upon completion of each **étape,** the realia may be used to review the functions, vocabulary, and grammar presented, or may be used as additional practice at any point within the **étape.** Along with the copying masters of the realia, you will find suggestions for using the realia in the classroom. These suggestions include a combination of activities for individual, pair, and group work which focus on the skills of listening, speaking, reading, writing, and explore authentic cultural information.

- **Situation Cards**   For each **étape** of the twelve chapters, three sets of interview questions and three situations for role-playing are provided as copying masters. These cards are designed to stimulate conversation and to prepare students for speaking tests. The interviews or role-playing may be used as pair work with the entire class, as activities to begin the class period, as oral performance assessment upon completion of the **étape,** or to encourage oral practice at any point during the **étape.** These conversations may be recorded as audio or video additions to students' portfolios. Because the cards may be recycled throughout the scholastic year to review chapters already completed, students will be rewarded as they realize they are meeting goals and improving their communicative abilities. To avoid having to copy the cards repeatedly, consider mounting them on cardboard and laminating them. They may be filed for use during the year as well as for future classes.

Communicative Activities

Nom_____ Classe_____ Date_____

Situation   You've just seen the person below leaving the scene of a crime.

Task   Describe what she was wearing and her physical features, so your partner, the police artist, can draw a picture of her.

EXEMPLE   — **La femme porte... Elle a les cheveux...**

LA SUSPECTE :

un jean
des bottes
un manteau
des chaussures
une jupe
des lunettes
un chemisier
un tee-shirt

Now you're the police artist. Draw the suspect your partner describes.

MON DESSIN :

French 2 Allez, viens!, Chapter 1

Activities for Communication **1**

Communicative Activity 1-1B

Situation   You're a police artist.

Task   Draw the picture of a suspect as your partner, the eyewitness, describes her.

MON DESSIN :

Now you're the eyewitness. Describe what the suspect was wearing and his physical features, so your partner, the police artist, can draw a picture of him.

EXEMPLE   — L'homme porte... Il a les cheveux...

LE SUSPECT :

un jean
des bottes
un manteau
des chaussures
une jupe
des lunettes
un chemisier
un tee-shirt

Situation   You're planning to visit several different cities in France.

Task   Ask your partner what the weather is like in each city listed below and what you should wear. Write down the information and advice your partner gives you.

EXEMPLE
— Quel temps fait-il à...?
— Il fait beau.
— Qu'est-ce que je dois mettre?
— Mets un jean et un tee-shirt.

LES VILLES :

	Il fait...	Je mets...
Paris :	_____	_____
Brest :	_____	_____
Nantes :	_____	_____
Nice :	_____	_____
Toulouse :	_____	_____

Now answer your partner's questions about the weather based on the map below and advise him or her what to wear.

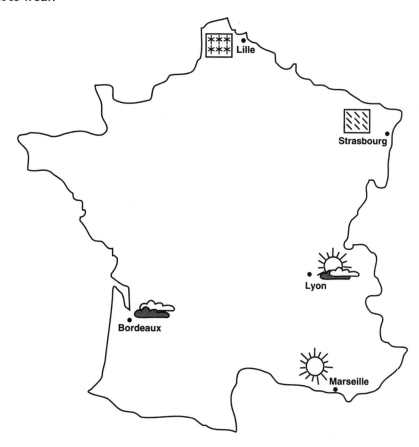

COMMUNICATIVE ACTIVITIES

Communicative Activity 1-2B

Situation Your partner is planning to visit the cities on the map below.

Task Answer his or her questions about the weather in each city and what he or she should wear.

EXEMPLE
— Quel temps fait-il à...?
— Il fait beau.
— Qu'est-ce que je dois mettre?
— Mets un jean et un tee-shirt.

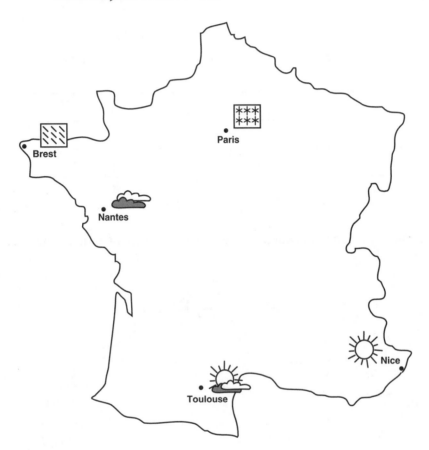

Now ask your partner what the weather is like in the cities listed below and what you should wear. Write down the information and advice your partner gives you.

LES VILLES :

	Il fait...	Je mets...
Lille :	_____	_____
Strasbourg :	_____	_____
Lyon :	_____	_____
Bordeaux :	_____	_____
Marseille :	_____	_____

French 2 Allez, viens!, Chapter 1

Communicative Activity 1-3A

1. Situation You and your partner are planning your next vacation together.

Task Your partner starts by asking what you should do. Using the expressions from the word box below and the cities on the list, suggest to your partner places you want to visit. Write down each of his or her responses on the line next to the place mentioned.

EXEMPLE — Qu'est-ce qu'on fait?
— On pourrait...
— Ça ne me dit rien.
— Bon, tu as envie de... ?

Si tu veux, on peut...   On pourrait...   Tu as envie de... ?   Ça te dit de... ?

1. aller à Los Angeles _____

2. aller à Miami _____

3. aller à Santa Fe _____

4. aller à Houston _____

5. aller à San Francisco _____

6. aller à Albuquerque _____

7. aller à Atlanta _____

8. aller à la Nouvelle-Orléans _____

Based on your partner's responses, tell him or her the itinerary for your vacation.
D'abord, ... Ensuite, ... Et puis, ... Finalement, ...

2. Now change roles. Ask your partner what you should do on vacation and respond to each suggestion your partner makes by using one of the phrases in the word box below.

D'accord.   Allons-y!   Ça ne me dit rien.

Je veux bien.   Pas question!

C'est une bonne/excellente idée.

Non, c'est...   Non, je préfère...

Communicative Activity 1-3B

COMMUNICATIVE ACTIVITIES

1. Situation You and your partner are planning your next vacation together.

Task Start the conversation by asking what you should do. Your partner will suggest places to visit. Respond to each suggestion using one of the expressions below.

EXEMPLE
— Qu'est-ce qu'on fait?
— On pourrait...
— Ça ne me dit rien.
— Bon, tu as envie de... ?

D'accord.   Allons-y!   Ça ne me dit rien.

Je veux bien.   Pas question!

C'est une bonne/excellente idée.

Non, c'est...   Non, je préfère...

2. Now change roles. Your partner will ask what you should do on vacation. Using the expressions from the box below and the countries on the list, suggest places you want to visit. Write down each of your partner's responses on the lines provided.

Si tu veux, on peut...   On pourrait...   Tu as envie de... ?   Ça te dit de... ?

1. aller en Espagne   _____

2. aller en France   _____

3. aller en Italie   _____

4. aller en Allemagne   _____

5. aller en Angleterre   _____

6. aller en Belgique   _____

7. aller en Suisse   _____

8. aller en Russie   _____

Based on your partner's responses, tell him or her the itinerary for your vacation.
D'abord, ... Ensuite, ... Et puis, ... Finalement, ...

1. Situation   You and your partner are catering a small party for some friends from school. Your partner has asked some of the guests what food items they want and you have asked the other guests. In order to prepare the right amount of food, you need to find out what all the guests would like to eat and drink.

Task   Ask your partner whether the guests on the list below are hungry or thirsty and check the appropriate blanks according to your partner's answers. Then write down the food items that each guest has asked for. When you have filled out your list, change roles with your partner.

EXEMPLE
— Est-ce que Joseph a faim?
— Non, il n'a pas faim.
— Est-ce qu'il a soif?
— Oui, il veut un coca.

Joseph _____ faim _____

      ✓ soif   un coca _____

Marie _____ faim _____

      _____ soif _____

Chantal _____ faim _____

      _____ soif _____

Malik _____ faim _____

      _____ soif _____

Eugène _____ faim _____

      _____ soif _____

2. Tell your partner whether each guest is hungry or thirsty and the food items he or she would like.

Yasmina	du jus de fruit
Pierre	rien
Boris	de la pizza
Françoise	un hot-dog, une limonade
Sandrine	une pâtisserie, un coca

Now tally all of the orders and compare pages with your partner to make sure you both have the same information.

limonade _____   coca _____   eau minérale _____   jus de fruit _____

pizza _____   hot-dog _____   pâtisserie _____

Communicative Activity 2-1B

1. Situation   You and your partner are catering a small party for some friends from school. Your partner has asked some of the guests what food items they want and you have asked the other guests. In order to prepare the right amount of food, you each need to find out what all the guests would like to eat and drink.

Task   Tell your partner whether the people on the list below are hungry or thirsty and what they would like. Your partner will write down your answers. Then ask your partner about the guests he or she spoke to.

EXEMPLE
— Est-ce que Joseph a faim?
— Non, il n'a pas faim.
— Est-ce qu'il a soif?
— Oui, il veut un coca.

Joseph	un coca
Marie	une pâtisserie, du jus de fruit
Chantal	rien
Malik	de la pizza, de l'eau minérale
Eugène	un hot-dog, une limonade

2. Check whether each guest is hungry or thirsty and write down the food items he or she would like.

Yasmina _____ faim   _____

_____ soif   _____

Pierre _____ faim   _____

_____ soif   _____

Boris _____ faim   _____

_____ soif   _____

Françoise _____ faim   _____

_____ soif   _____

Sandrine _____ faim   _____

_____ soif   _____

Now tally all of the orders and compare pages with your partner to make sure you both have the same information.

limonade _____   coca _____   eau minérale _____   jus de fruit _____

pizza _____   hot-dog _____   pâtisserie _____

French 2 Allez, viens!, Chapter 2

Nom_____ Classe_____ Date_____

Situation Imagine that this is your bedroom pictured below. Your partner has identical furniture in his or her room, but it's arranged differently.

Task Ask your partner where each piece of furniture is located in his or her room and draw it on the sketch at the bottom of your paper. Then your partner will ask you where the same piece of furniture is located in your room. Take turns asking questions. When you've finished, compare your drawings to see if they match.

EXEMPLE — **Dans ta chambre, où est le tapis?**
— **Il est devant la fenêtre. Et dans ta chambre?**
— **Dans ma chambre, le tapis est devant mon lit.**

MA CHAMBRE :

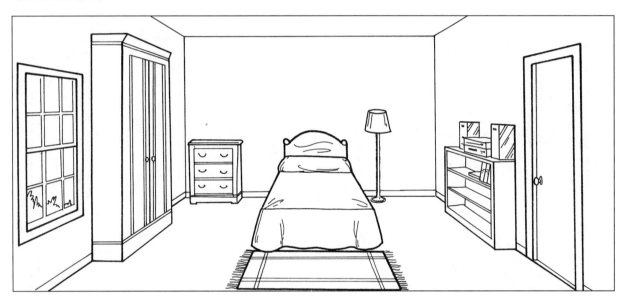

LA CHAMBRE DE MON/MA CAMARADE :

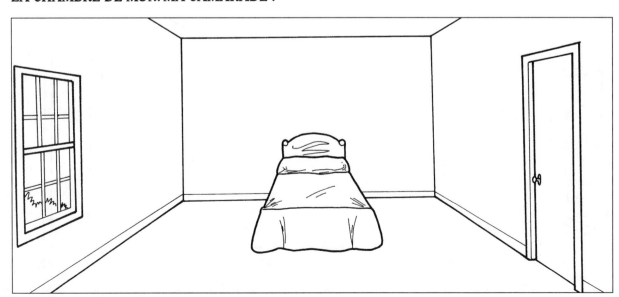

Activities for Communication **9**

Communicative Activity 2-2B

Situation Imagine that this is your bedroom pictured below. Your partner has identical furniture in his or her room, but it's arranged differently than in your room.

Task Your partner will ask you where each piece of furniture is located in your bedroom. Then ask your partner where the same piece of furniture is located in his or her room and draw it on the sketch at the bottom of your paper. Take turns asking questions. When you've finished, compare your drawings to see if they match.

EXEMPLE — **Dans ta chambre, où est le tapis?**
— **Il est devant la fenêtre. Et dans ta chambre?**
— **Dans ma chambre, le tapis est devant mon lit.**

MA CHAMBRE :

LA CHAMBRE DE MON/MA CAMARADE :

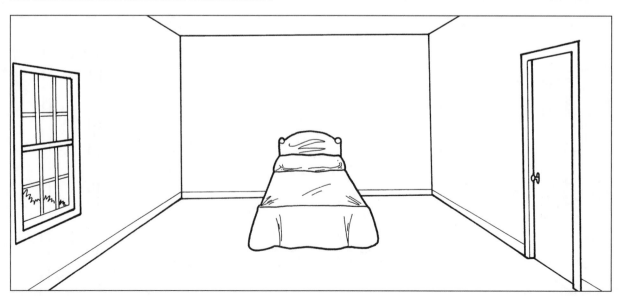

French 2 Allez, viens!, Chapter 2

Situation   You're about to go on a tour of the town below, but your map isn't complete. You decide to ask a passer-by how to get to the places you want to go.

Task   Ask your partner for directions to each of the places listed below. Listen to the directions and trace on your map the route he or she describes. When you reach your destination, write in the name of the place on the space provided. Once you have located all the places on your list, change roles. When you've given directions to all the places your partner asks about, compare maps to see if you have the same information.

EXEMPLE   — Où est l'auberge de jeunesse, s'il vous plaît?
  — Prenez la rue de la Gare. Ensuite,...

Tu es...	Tu veux aller...
1. à la gare.	à l'auberge de jeunesse.
2. à l'auberge de jeunesse.	à la poste.
3. à la poste.	au restaurant.

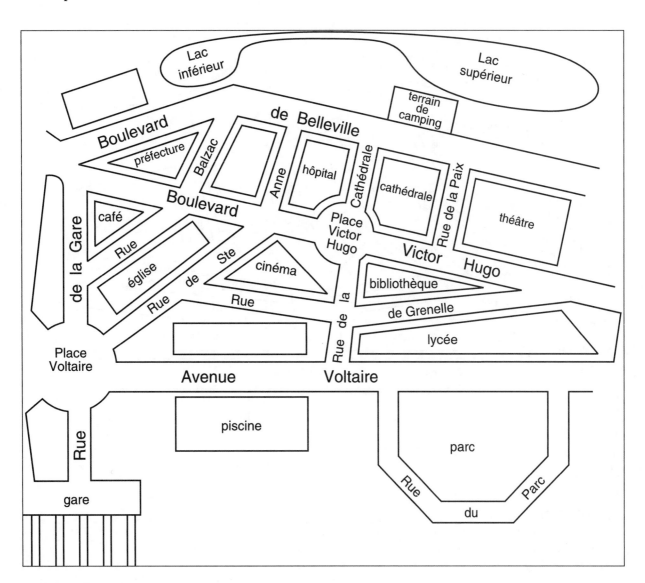

Communicative Activity 2-3B

Situation Your partner is about to go on a tour of the town below, but his or her map isn't complete. Your partner decides to ask you how to get to the places he or she wants to go.

Task Give your partner directions to the places he or she asks about. Then change roles. Ask your partner how to get to each of the places listed below. Listen to the directions and trace on your map the route he or she describes. When you reach your destination, write in the name of the place on the space provided. Once you've located all the places on your list, compare maps with your partner to see if you have the same information.

EXEMPLE — Où est le terrain de camping, s'il vous plaît?
— Prenez la rue de la Gare. Ensuite,...

Tu es...	Tu veux aller...
1. à la gare.	au terrain de camping.
2. au terrain de camping.	au théâtre.
3. au théâtre.	au café.

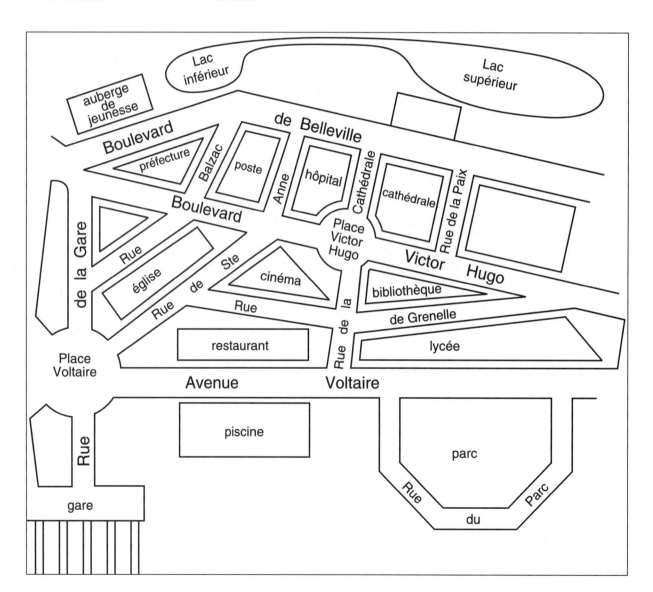

Situation   You and your partner are planning a dinner party. To decide what to serve, you've asked several of your friends what they like and don't like to eat, and your partner has asked others.

Task   Ask what each friend on your list likes or dislikes according to the spaces on your chart which need to be filled in. Take turns asking questions with your partner until you've both filled in all the blank spaces on your charts. When you've finished, compare your papers to make sure you have the same information.

EXEMPLE   — Qu'est-ce que Mireille aime comme plat principal?
                 — Elle aime le bifteck et le poisson.

	Entrée		Plat principal	
	aime	**n'aime pas**	**aime**	**n'aime pas**
Mireille	crevettes, pâté	escargots		
Séka	pâté			poisson
Van	pâté	huîtres		poisson, rôti de porc
Fatima			tout	
Frédéric		escargots	bœuf	poisson
Nabil				

Based on what you've learned about everyone's likes and dislikes, what do you recommend preparing for dinner? Write in French what you think you should serve and what you definitely should not serve for the appetizer and the main dish.

_____

_____

_____

_____

_____

COMMUNICATIVE ACTIVITIES

 Communicative Activity 3-1B

Situation You and your partner are planning a dinner party. To decide what to serve, you've asked several of your friends what they like and what they don't like to eat, and your partner has asked others.

Task Ask what each friend on your list likes or dislikes according to the spaces on your chart which need to be filled in. Take turns asking questions with your partner until you've both filled in all the blank spaces on your charts. When you've finished, compare your papers to make sure you have the same information.

EXEMPLE
— Qu'est-ce que Mireille aime comme entrée?
— Elle aime les crevettes et le pâté.

	Entrée		Plat principal	
	aime	n'aime pas	aime	n'aime pas
Mireille			bifteck, poisson	poulet
Séka		crevettes	bifteck	
Van			poulet, bifteck	
Fatima	huîtres, pâté	crevettes		rôti de bœuf
Frédéric	huîtres			
Nabil	pâté	escargots	tout	poisson

Based on what you've learned about everyone's likes and dislikes, what do you recommend preparing for dinner? Write in French what you think you should serve and what you definitely should not serve for the appetizer and the main dish.

_____

_____

_____

_____

_____

Situation   You have a lot of errands to do to prepare for a birthday party you're giving this weekend.

Task   Ask your partner if he or she can stop by the places illustrated below. When your partner agrees, ask him or her to buy the item given under each illustration. Then your partner will ask you to run some errands. Write down the name of the store and what your partner wants you to buy there. When you've finished, compare your papers to see if you have the same information.

EXEMPLE   — **Tu pourrais passer à... ?**
                     — **Oui, ...**
                     — **Tu pourrais acheter (me rapporter)... ?**
                     — **Oui, et quoi d'autre?**

LES COURSES DE MON/MA CAMARADE :

du fromage

un gâteau au chocolat

500 grammes de pâté

des disques compacts

un kilo de crevettes

MES COURSES :

_____
_____

_____
_____

_____
_____

_____
_____

_____
_____

Communicative Activity 3-2B

Situation Your partner wants you to help prepare for a birthday party he or she is planning. He or she will ask you to run some errands.

Task Write down the name of the store and what your partner wants you to buy there. Then ask your partner for help with a party you're planning. Ask your partner if he or she can stop by the places illustrated at the bottom of your paper. When your partner agrees, ask him or her to buy the item given under each illustration. When you've finished, compare your papers to see if you have the same information.

EXEMPLE
— Tu pourrais passer à... ?
— Oui, ...
— Tu pourrais acheter (me rapporter)... ?
— Oui, et quoi d'autre?

MES COURSES :

_____
_____

_____
_____

_____
_____

_____
_____

_____
_____

LES COURSES DE MON/MA CAMARADE :

quatre baguettes

six biftecks

des fruits

une douzaine d'œufs et un litre de lait

trois litres de coca

French 2 Allez, viens!, Chapter 3

1. Situation You and your partner are planning to do some holiday shopping. You already have a short list of gifts to buy for your family, but your partner wants to make some other suggestions.

Task Tell your partner what gifts you might offer to each of the family members on your list below. He or she will agree with one of your ideas or make another suggestion. If the item your partner suggests is not on your list, accept or reject the advice, using expressions in the word box to vary your conversation. Then change roles.

EXEMPLE
— Je vais offrir... à ma sœur.
— Bonne idée, offre-lui...

or

— Je vais offrir... à ma sœur.
— Pourquoi pas lui offrir...
— C'est original! *or* Non, ce n'est pas son style.

a. MA SŒUR
un foulard
des bonbons

b. MA TANTE
un poster
une vase

c. MES GRANDS-PARENTS
un cadre
des fleurs

d. MA COUSINE
un cadre
un vase

e. MON ONCLE
une cravate
une boîte de chocolats

f. MES PARENTS
des CD
des livres

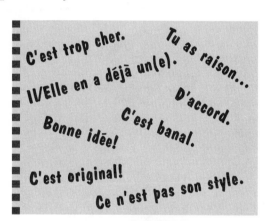

C'est trop cher.
Tu as raison...
Il/Elle en a déjà un(e).
D'accord.
Bonne idée!
C'est banal.
C'est original!
Ce n'est pas son style.

2. Now your partner will tell you what gifts he or she is planning to buy for his or her family members. If the pictures below match an item on your partner's list, agree with the matching item. If not, offer a new suggestion based on the picture you have.

a.

b.

c.

d.

e.

f.

Communicative Activity 3-3B

1. **Situation**   You and your partner are planning to do some holiday shopping. Your partner already has a short list of gifts he or she could offer to various family members, but you want to make some other suggestions.

   Task   Your partner will tell you what he or she is planning to buy for various family members. If the picture you have matches an item on your partner's list, agree with the matching item. If not, make a new suggestion based on the picture you have below. Your partner will accept or refuse the advice. Then change roles.

   EXEMPLE
   — Je vais offrir... à ma sœur.
   — Bonne idée, offre-lui...
   or
   — Je vais offrir... à ma sœur.
   — Pourquoi pas lui offrir...
   — C'est original! *or* Non, ce n'est pas son style.

a.

b.

c.

d.

e.

f.

2. Now tell your partner what gifts you are planning to buy for each of the family members on your list below. Your partner will agree with one of your ideas, or make another suggestion. Accept or reject the advice, using expressions in the word box to vary your conversation.

> C'est trop cher.   Tu as raison...
> Il/Elle en a déjà un(e).   D'accord.
> Bonne idée!   C'est banal.
> C'est original!
> Ce n'est pas son style.

a. MON GRAND-PERE
   un poster
   un CD

b. MON FRERE
   une cravate
   des CD

c. MON COUSIN
   un poster
   un livre

d. MA COUSINE
   des fleurs
   un sac à main

e. MON ONCLE ET MA TANTE
   un cadre
   une boîte de chocolats

f. MES PARENTS
   des fleurs
   des bonbons

French 2 Allez, viens!, Chapter 3

*Nom*_____ *Classe*_____ *Date*_____

Situation   You and your partner are preparing a report on Martinique. You want to show where certain features are located on the map. You have information on the first four features shown on the bottom of the page, and your partner has information on the last four.

Task   Take turns asking where certain features are located and then drawing them on your map. When you've finished, compare papers to make sure you have the same information on your maps.

EXEMPLE   — Où est-ce qu'il y a des bananiers?
                           — Il y a des bananiers...

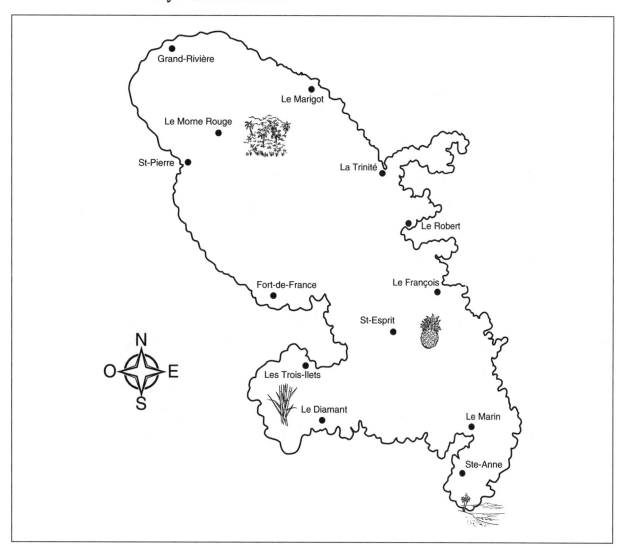

Activities for Communication **19**

COMMUNICATIVE ACTIVITIES

Communicative Activity 4-1B

Situation   You and your partner are preparing a report on Martinique. You want to show where certain features are located on the map. You have information on the last four features shown on the bottom of the page, and your partner has information on the first four.

Task   Take turns asking where certain features are located and then drawing them on your map. When you've finished, compare papers to make sure you have the same information on your maps.

EXEMPLE   — Où est-ce qu'il y a un champ d'ananas?
                   — Il y a un champ d'ananas...

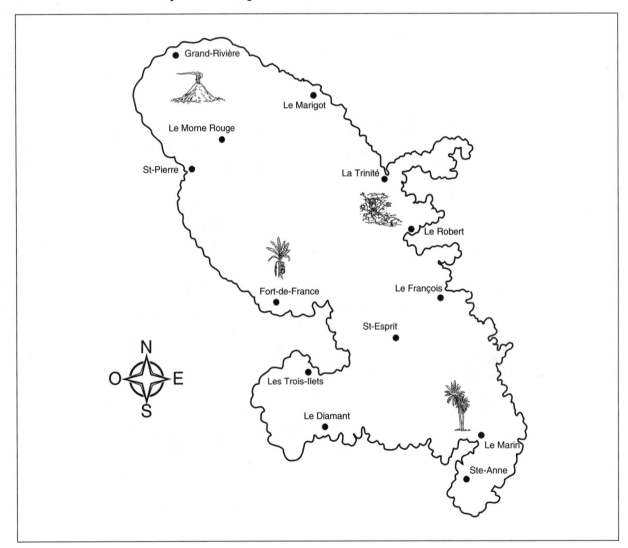

Situation   You're visiting your pen pal (your partner) in Martinique. He or she has a very busy schedule planned for you.

Task   Ask what you're going to do first, next, and so on, and number the pictures accordingly. Then change roles and answer your partner's questions, telling in what order you've planned to do the activities pictured at the bottom of your paper.

EXEMPLE   — Qu'est-ce qu'on fait d'abord?
                     — D'abord, on va à la pêche.
                     — Et après?

MES PROJETS :

LES PROJETS POUR MON/MA CAMARADE :

1.   2.   3.

4.   5.

COMMUNICATIVE ACTIVITIES

Communicative Activity 4-2B

Situation Your pen pal (your partner) is visiting you in Martinique. You have a very busy schedule planned.

Task Answer your partner's questions about the order of the activities you've planned, based on the pictures below. Then change roles and ask your partner what you're going to do first, next, and so on, and number the pictures at the bottom of your paper accordingly.

EXEMPLE
— Qu'est-ce qu'on fait d'abord?
— D'abord, on va à la pêche.
— Et après?

LES PROJETS POUR MON/MA CAMARADE :

1.

2.

3.

4.

5.

MES PROJETS :

French 2 Allez, viens!, Chapter 4

1. **Situation** You've just arrived at your host family's home in Martinique. In order to establish your daily routine, you need to find out the routine of your new family members.

   Task Ask your partner about the routine of the family members listed below. Fill out the schedule with the information your partner gives you.

   EXEMPLE   — **Quelle est la routine de... ?**
   — **D'abord, il/elle se lève à... ensuite,... finalement,...**

	se lever	se laver	aller travailler/ aller au lycée	dîner	se coucher
Mme Régis					
M. Régis					
Jules					
Jim					

   Now tell what your daily routine is going to be, based on the information you have about your host family.

   D'abord, je vais me lever à...

2. Change roles. Now imagine that you're a member of the host family for an exchange student who has just arrived at your home in Martinique. Answer the questions your partner asks you based on the information below.

	se lever	se laver	aller travailler/ aller au lycée	dîner	se coucher
Mme Condé	6h	6h30	7h15	19h	22h
M. Condé	6h30	7h	8h30	19h	22h30
Lucie	7h	7h30	8h30	19h	21h30
Félix	7h	8h	8h30	19h	22h30

Communicative Activity 4-3B

1. **Situation**   Imagine that you're a member of the host family for an exchange student who has just arrived at your home in Martinique. In order to get settled in, the exchange student (your partner) asks some questions about your family's daily routine.

   Task   Answer your partner's questions based on the information below.

   EXEMPLE   — Quelle est la routine de... ?
   — D'abord, il/elle se lève à... ensuite,... finalement,...

	se lever	se laver	aller travailler/ aller au lycée	dîner	se coucher
Mme Régis	5h30	5h45	8h30	18h30	22h
M. Régis	6h	6h15	7h	18h30	23h
Jules	6h30	6h45	7h30	18h30	21h
Jim	6h30	7h	7h30	18h30	21h

2. Change roles. Now you're an exchange student who has just arrived at your host family's home in Martinique. In order to establish your daily routine, ask about the routine of the family members listed below. Fill in the information your partner tells you.

	se lever	se laver	aller travailler/ aller au lycée	dîner	se coucher
Mme Condé					
M. Condé					
Lucie					
Félix					

Now tell what your daily routine is going to be, based on the information you have about your host family.

D'abord, je vais me lever à...

Situation   You want to know what your partner did today.

Task   Ask your partner what he or she did today, using connecting words like **d'abord, ensuite,** and so on. Number the pictured activities from 1 to 5 in the order in which your partner did them. Then answer your partner's questions about your day, according to the illustrations at the bottom of your paper. When you've finished, compare papers to be sure you have the same information.

EXEMPLE   — Qu'est-ce que tu as fait, d'abord?
                         — . . .
                         — Et ensuite?

LA JOURNEE DE MON/MA CAMARADE :

MA JOURNEE :

1.    **2.**    **3.**

4.    **5.**

Communicative Activity 5-1B

COMMUNICATIVE ACTIVITIES

Situation Your partner wants to know what you did today.

Task Answer his or her questions, according to the activities pictured below. Then ask your partner about his or her day, using connecting words like **d'abord, ensuite,** and so on. Number the pictured activities at the bottom of your page from 1 to 5 in the order in which your partner did them. When you've finished, compare papers to be sure you have the same information.

EXEMPLE
— Qu'est-ce que tu as fait, d'abord?
— . . .
— Et ensuite?

MA JOURNEE :

1.

2.

3.

4.

5.

LA JOURNEE DE MON/MA CAMARADE :

_____

_____

_____

_____

_____

French 2 Allez, viens!, Chapter 5

Communicative Activity 5-2A

1. **Situation** You want to know how your partner's classes went yesterday.

   Task Ask your partner how his or her classes went yesterday and what happened. Write his or her responses in the spaces provided.

   EXEMPLE   — **Comment ça s'est passé hier en maths?**
   — **En maths, pas très bien.**
   — **Pourquoi?**
   — **Je n'ai pas fait mes devoirs.**
   ...

   LES COURS DE MON/MA CAMARADE :

COURS	Ça s'est passé...	Pourquoi?/Raconte!
maths		
français		
sciences nat		
EPS		
anglais		
histoire		

2. Now fill in the chart below with information about your courses. Then answer your partner's questions about how your classes went yesterday and what happened. When you've finished, compare papers to be sure you each have the same information.

   MES COURS :

COURS	Ça s'est passé...	Pourquoi?/Raconte!
maths		
anglais		
français		
géographie		
arts plastiques		
informatique		

COMMUNICATIVE ACTIVITIES

Communicative Activity 5-2B

1. Situation   Your partner wants to know how your classes went yesterday and why.

Task   Fill in the chart below with information about your courses. Then answer your partner's questions about how your classes went yesterday and what happened.

EXEMPLE   — **Comment ça s'est passé hier en maths?**
                   — **En maths, pas très bien.**
                   — **Pourquoi?**
                   — **Je n'ai pas fait mes devoirs.**
                       ...

MES COURS :

COURS	Ça s'est passé...	Pourquoi?/Raconte!
maths		
français		
sciences nat		
EPS		
anglais		
histoire		

2. Now ask your partner questions about how his or her classes went yesterday and what happened. When you've finished, compare papers to be sure you have the same information.

LES COURS DE MON/MA CAMARADE :

COURS	Ça s'est passé...	Pourquoi?/Raconte!
maths		
anglais		
français		
géographie		
arts plastiques		
informatique		

French 2 Allez, viens!, Chapter 5

1. Situation   You and your brother or sister have found report cards belonging to your parents. The cards show that they had the same classes. The teachers' comments are missing on both.

Task   Ask your partner what grades your father received for each of the subjects on his report card. Use your mother's report card on the bottom of the page to see which subjects to ask about. Your partner will tell you the grade. Then choose an appropriate comment (congratulation, encouragement, or reprimand) from the word box below. Try to use each expression only once.

EXEMPLE   — Combien est-ce qu'il a eu en maths?
                     — Il a eu 6.
                     — Il doit mieux travailler en classe.

> Elève très sérieux.   Résultats encourageants.   C'est inadmissible!
>
>   Bravo!
>
> Il a fait beaucoup de progrès.   Il doit mieux travailler en classe.   Courage!
>
> Satisfaisant.   Formidable!
>   Il ne doit pas faire le clown en classe.

2. Change roles. Your partner will ask what grades your mother received for each of the subjects on the report card. Tell the grade your mother received. Then your partner will offer appropriate comments. Fill in his or her comments.

Le bulletin de ta mère :

Matières	Moyenne	Appréciations
Maths	10	
Français	15	
Sc. physiques	8	
Sc. naturelles	14	
Histoire-Géographie	12	
Anglais	15	
Latin	11	
Education physique	9	

Now compare the completed report cards. Decide which parent you are most like and give the reasons.

Je ressemble à… parce que…

Communicative Activity 5-3B

1. **Situation** You and your brother or sister have found report cards belonging to your parents. The cards show that they had the same classes. The teachers' comments are missing on both.

   Task Your partner will ask what grades your father received for each of the subjects on his report card. Tell him or her the grade. Then your partner will offer an appropriate comment (congratulation, encouragement, or reprimand). Write down his or her comments.

   EXEMPLE   — Combien est-ce qu'il a eu en maths?
                   — Il a eu 6.
                   — Il doit mieux travailler en classe.

   Le bulletin de ton père :

Matières	Moyenne	Appréciations
Maths	6	
Français	11	
Sc. physiques	16	
Sc. naturelles	9	
Histoire-Géographie	16	
Anglais	7	
Latin	15	
Education physique	13	

2. Change roles. Ask your partner what grades your mother received for each of the subjects on the report card. Use your father's card to see which subjects to ask about. Your partner will tell you the grade. Then choose an appropriate comment from the word box below. Try to use each expression only once.

   Elève très sérieuse.   Elle a fait beaucoup de progrès.   Félicitations!

   Courage!

   C'est inadmissible!   Elle doit mieux travailler en classe.   Bravo!

   Travail moyen.   Elle ne doit pas faire le clown en classe.   Chapeau!

   Now compare the completed report cards. Decide which parent you are most like and give the reasons.

   Je ressemble à… parce que…

COMMUNICATIVE ACTIVITIES

1. **Situation**   A group of your friends went to visit a castle in the Loire region of France. Unfortunately, you weren't able to join them, but you're very curious about the trip.
   Task   Ask your partner the questions below. Write the information in the spaces provided.

   1. Quel château avez-vous visité? _____

   2. Combien de personnes y sont allées? _____

   3. C'était combien, l'entrée? _____

   4. Pourquoi est-ce que Catherine est allée à la boutique de souvenirs? _____

   5. Qu'est-ce que vous avez fait le soir? _____

   6. A quelle heure avez-vous pris le bus pour rentrer? _____

   7. C'était comment? _____

2. You were able to tour the castle of Loches with a group of your friends. Answer your partner's questions about the visit according to the pictures below.

Communicative Activity 6-1B

1. **Situation**   You and a group of your friends went to visit the Chenonceau castle in the Loire region of France. Your partner wasn't able to join the group and wants to know all about the trip.

   Task   Answer his or her questions according to the pictures below.

2. Your partner went on a tour of a castle in the Loire region. Ask the following questions about his or her trip and write the information in the spaces provided.

   1. Quel château avez-vous visité? _____

   2. Combien de personnes y sont allées? _____

   3. C'était combien, l'entrée? _____

   4. Qu'est-ce que Mathieu a acheté comme souvenir? _____

   5. Est-ce que vous êtes montés dans la vieille tour? _____

   6. Est-ce que vous avez fait un pique-nique? _____

   7. C'était comment? _____

1. **Situation** You and your partner have discovered some photos from your grandmother's trip to Paris in the 1960s. You are trying to put the photos in order according to the information in her journal.

   Task Ask your partner what your grandmother did on each day of the week. Match the activity your partner describes with a photo on your page. Then write the day of the week under the correct photo. When you've finished the first week, change roles.

   EXEMPLE — Qu'est-ce qu'elle a fait lundi?
   — Lundi, elle est arrivée à Paris à l'aéroport d'Orly.

   La première semaine à Paris :

_____ _____ _____

_____ _____ _____ _____

2. Tell your partner which activity your grandmother did on each day of the week according to her journal.

   La deuxième semaine à Paris :

   Paris, mai 1965

   Lundi, j'ai eu un accident. Je suis tombée devant la Basilique du Sacré-Cœur.

   Mardi, je suis restée au lit, à l'hôtel.

   Mercredi, je suis sortie avec des amis et nous sommes allés à l'Opéra.

   Jeudi, j'ai fait une visite guidée de Notre-Dame.

   Vendredi, je suis partie pour Versailles où j'ai vu la galerie des Glaces.

   Samedi, j'ai acheté beaucoup de souvenirs pour ma famille.

   Dimanche, je suis rentrée aux États-Unis.

   Now compare papers with your partner to make sure you have the same information.

Communicative Activity 6-2B

1. Situation You and your partner have discovered some photos from your grandmother's trip to Paris in the 1960s. You are trying to put the photos in order according to the information in her journal.

Task Tell your partner what your grandmother did on each day of the week, according to the information in her journal. When you've finished the first week, change roles.

EXEMPLE — Qu'est-ce qu'elle a fait lundi?
— Lundi, elle est arrivée à Paris à l'aéroport d'Orly.

La première semaine à Paris :

Paris, mai 1965

Lundi, je suis arrivée à Paris à l'aéroport d'Orly.

Mardi, je suis allée au Louvre et j'ai vu la Joconde.

Mercredi, je suis montée dans la tour Eiffel et j'ai vu tout Paris.

Jeudi, je suis allée dans un très bon restaurant.

Vendredi, j'ai fait du shopping dans une boutique très chic.

Samedi, je suis partie pour Chartres.

Dimanche, je suis retournée à Paris.

2. Ask your partner what your grandmother did on each day of the week during her second week in Paris. Match the activity your partner describes to one of the photos below and fill in the day of the week under the correct photo.

_____   _____   _____

_____   _____   _____   _____

Now compare papers with your partner to make sure you have the same information.

French 2 Allez, viens!, Chapter 6

Communicative Activity 6-3A

Situation   You and your partner are in Paris. You'd like to visit another city, so you're looking at train schedules.

Task   Ask your partner for the information that is missing from your schedule. Then answer your partner's questions, giving the information you have on your schedule. Take turns. When you've finished, compare papers to make sure you have the same information.

EXEMPLE

— **A quelle heure est-ce que le train arrive à Nice?**
— **A...**

— **De quel quai est-ce qu'il part?**
— **Du quai...**

— **Combien coûte un aller-retour pour Bruxelles?**
— **... euros.**

HORAIRE				
De Paris à...	Départ	Arrivée	Tarif (A/R)	Quai
Nice	6h45		145 €	
Honfleur		12h04	72 €	3
Bruxelles		12h51		
Annecy	11h29			5
Marseille		21h57		2
Deauville		18h45		
Genève	18h57		118 €	10
Font-Romeu	19h32		122 €	

Communicative Activity 6-3B

Situation   You and your partner are in Paris. You'd like to visit another city, so you're looking at train schedules.

Task   Answer your partner's questions, giving the information you have on your schedule. Then ask your partner for the information that is missing from your schedule. Take turns. When you've finished, compare papers to make sure you have the same information.

EXEMPLE
— **A quelle heure est-ce que le train part pour Nice?**
— **A...**

— **De quel quai est-ce qu'il part?**
— **Du quai...**

— **Combien coûte un aller-retour pour Nice?**
— **... euros.**

HORAIRE				
De Paris à...	Départ	Arrivée	Tarif (A/R)	Quai
Nice		14h10		1
Honfleur	7h11			
Bruxelles	8h49		115 €	4
Annecy		16h03	80 €	
Marseille	14h58		130 €	
Deauville	15h30		32 €	7
Genève		23h48		
Font-Romeu		0h10		3

French 2 Allez, viens!, Chapter 6

1. Situation   You and your partner are helping the school nurse update the patients' charts and there are a lot of ailing students.

   Task   Ask your partner what is wrong with the patients listed in the chart below and record their ailments.

   EXEMPLE   — Qu'est-ce qu'elle a, Marie-Claire?
                        — Elle a le nez qui coule.

   LES PATIENTS DE MON/MA CAMARADE :

PATIENT(E)	PROBLEME DE SANTE
Marie-Claire	_____
Mona	_____
Daniel	_____
Li	_____
Siméon	_____

2. Now your partner will ask you about the patients on his or her list. Answer his or her questions according to the pictures below. When you've finished, compare papers to make sure you have the same information.

   MES PATIENTS :

Séka

Jean-Luc

Simone

Renée

Van

French 2 Allez, viens!, Chapter 7

Communicative Activity 7-1B

1. **Situation**   You and your partner are helping the school nurse update the patients' charts and there are a lot of ailing students.

   Task   Your partner will ask you about the people on his or her list. Answer his or her questions according to the pictures below.

MES PATIENTS :

Marie-Claire

Mona

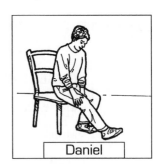
Daniel

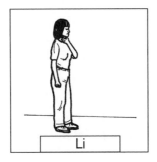
Li

Siméon

2. Now, ask your partner about the patients listed in the chart below and record their ailments. When you've finished, compare papers to make sure you have the same information.

   EXEMPLE   — Qu'est-ce qu'il a, Séka?
                        — Il a mal aux dents.

   LES PATIENTS DE MON/MA CAMARADE :

PATIENT(E)	PROBLEME DE SANTE
Séka	_____
Jean-Luc	_____
Simone	_____
Renée	_____
Van	_____

Situation You and your partner are playing a game.

Task Ask your partner if he or she does one of the activities listed on your game board. Then write **oui** or **non** in the space provided according to his or her response. Take turns asking questions. The winner is the first person to connect four squares of all **oui** or all **non** answers vertically, horizontally, or diagonally.

EXEMPLE 　　　　— **Tu fais du ski?**
　　　　　　　　— **Oui.**
　　　　　　　　or
　　　　　　　　— **Tu vas au cinéma?**
　　　　　　　　— **Non.**

faire du ski	aller à la pêche	faire les devoirs	aller au cinéma
_____	_____	_____	_____
boire du lait	faire du vélo	s'entraîner au volley	jouer au basket
_____	_____	_____	_____
aller à des boums	faire de la natation	jouer au football américain	faire des pompes
_____	_____	_____	_____
faire de la musculation	faire de la gymnastique	faire des abdominaux	faire de l'aérobic
_____	_____	_____	_____

COMMUNICATIVE ACTIVITIES

 Communicative Activity 7-2B

Situation   You and your partner are playing a game.

Task   Your partner will ask you if you do a certain activity. Answer, then ask your partner if he or she does an activity listed on your game board. Write **oui** or **non** in the space provided according to his or her response. Take turns asking questions. The winner is the first person to connect four squares of all **oui** or all **non** answers vertically, horizontally, or diagonally.

EXEMPLE
— **Tu fais du ski?**
— **Oui.**
or
— **Tu vas au cinéma?**
— **Non.**

faire du vélo	jouer au basket	faire de la natation	aller à des boums
_____	_____	_____	_____
aller à la pêche	faire du ski	jouer au football américain	faire des pompes
_____	_____	_____	_____
faire de la gymnastique	faire de l'aérobic	aller au cinéma	faire les devoirs
_____	_____	_____	_____
boire du lait	s'entraîner au hockey	faire de la musculation	faire des abdominaux
_____	_____	_____	_____

Nom _____ Classe _____ Date _____

1. **Situation**   You and your health-conscious partner are buying groceries at a French supermarket.
   Task   Tell your partner which items you would like to buy, based on the illustrations below.
   Your partner will either agree with your recommendation or advise against it. Place a check-
   mark below each item your partner agrees to buy.
   EXEMPLE   — Je voudrais acheter des chips.
                       — Non, on ne doit pas consommer trop de matières grasses.

2. Change roles. Now your partner will tell what he or she wants to buy at the supermarket. Agree
   or disagree with his or her recommendations using expressions from the word box below.

Oui...	Non...
C'est bon pour la santé.	Il faut éviter de...
Ça nous fera du bien.	On ne devrait pas...
On doit manger...	On doit éviter de consommer trop de...

Now create with your partner a complete list of the food items you both agree to buy.

_____

_____

_____

_____

_____

_____

COMMUNICATIVE ACTIVITIES

Communicative Activity 7-3B

1. **Situation** You and your partner are buying groceries at a French supermarket. You are very health conscious.

   Task Your partner will tell you which items he or she would like to buy at the supermarket. Agree or disagree with his or her recommendations using expressions from the word box below.

   EXEMPLE — Je voudrais acheter des chips.
   — Non, on ne doit pas consommer trop de matières grasses.

Oui...	Non...
C'est bon pour la santé.	Il faut éviter de...
Ça nous fera du bien.	On ne devrait pas...
On doit manger...	On doit éviter de consommer trop de...

2. Change roles. Now tell your partner which items you would like to buy based on the illustrations below. Your partner will agree with your recommendation or advise against it. Place a checkmark below each item your partner agrees to buy.

Now create with your partner a complete list of the food items you both agree to buy.

_____

_____

_____

_____

_____

_____

French 2 Allez, viens!, Chapter 7

Situation   You and your partner are writing an article for the French Club newspaper about the club members' most recent vacations. You interviewed half of the students on the list of members and your partner interviewed the other half.

Task   Ask your partner where the students he or she interviewed went on their last vacations and what it was like there. Write down the information. Then tell your partner about the students you interviewed, based on the information at the bottom of the page.

EXEMPLE
— **Georges est allé où pour les vacances?**
— **Il est allé...**
— **C'était comment?**
— **C'était...**

Liste d'élèves :

	est allé(e)...	C'était...
Georges		
Marie		
Joëlle		
Francine		
Benjamin		
Elodie		

Aminata	Paris	très vivant, bruyant
Félix	Paris	stressant, nul
Prosper	Québec	tranquille, calme
Sandrine	Fort-de-France	magnifique, très vivant
Aïcha	Abidjan	animé, génial
Pascal	Abidjan	bruyant, stressant

COMMUNICATIVE ACTIVITIES

 Communicative Activity 8-1B

Situation   You and your partner are writing an article for the French Club newspaper about the club members' most recent vacations. You interviewed half of the students on the list of members and your partner interviewed the other half.

Task   Tell your partner where the students you interviewed went on their last vacations and what it was like there. Then ask your partner about the students he or she interviewed and write down the information.

EXEMPLE
— Georges est allé où pour les vacances?
— Il est allé...
— C'était comment?
— C'était...

Liste d'élèves :

	est allé(e)...	C'était...
Georges	Abidjan	très vivant, animé
Marie	Québec	calme, propre
Joëlle	Québec	très relaxant, tranquille
Francine	Paris	animé, dangereux
Benjamin	Abidjan	bruyant, très vivant
Elodie	Fort-de-France	tranquille, calme

Aminata		
Félix		
Prosper		
Sandrine		
Aïcha		
Pascal		

French 2 Allez, viens!, Chapter 8

1. **Situation**   You're a famous artist. You've been commissioned to make a sketch of a childhood friend your client remembers. He or she would like the boy to be shown doing his favorite activity in front of the house where he used to live. There's no photo available, so you have to rely on your client's description.

   Task   Draw the boy as your client (your partner) describes him.

   MON DESSIN :

2. Change roles. You've decided to commission an artist to make a sketch of a friend you recall from your childhood. Describe the girl pictured below to the artist (your partner), who will draw her.

Communicative Activity 8-2B

1. **Situation**   You've decided to commission an artist to make a sketch of a childhood friend you remember. Unfortunately, there's no photo available, so you'll have to describe your friend to the artist (your partner).

   Task   Describe the boy pictured below to the artist (your partner) who will draw him.

2. Change roles. You're a famous artist. You've been commissioned to make a sketch of a childhood friend your client remembers. He or she would like the girl to be shown doing her favorite activity in front of the house where she used to live. There's no photo available, so you have to rely on your client's description. Draw the girl as your client (your partner) describes her.

MON DESSIN :

Situation You and your partner are deciding what to do in Abidjan.

Task Suggest the activities pictured below. Write down your partner's response in the space below each picture. Then respond to your partner's suggestions illustrated at the bottom of your paper.

EXEMPLE
— **Si on jouait au foot?**
— **D'accord.**

MES SUGGESTIONS :

_____

_____

_____

LES SUGGESTIONS DE MON/MA CAMARADE :

Now write down what the two of you decided to do.

_____

_____

_____

_____

_____

Communicative Activity 8-3B

Situation You and your partner are deciding what to do in Abidjan.

Task Respond to your partner's suggestions pictured below. Then suggest the activities pictured at the bottom of your paper. Write down your partner's response in the space below each picture.

EXEMPLE — Si on achetait des poteries?
— Bof. Ça ne me dit rien.

LES SUGGESTIONS DE MON/MA CAMARADE :

MES SUGGESTIONS :

_____ _____ _____ _____

_____ _____ _____ _____

_____ _____ _____ _____

Now write down what the two of you decided to do.

_____

_____

_____

_____

_____

French 2 Allez, viens!, Chapter 8

1. **Situation**   You went to a party last weekend, and your partner wants to hear all about it.

   Task   Look at the group photo below and tell your partner how each guest was feeling. After each description, your partner will offer a possible explanation for the person's mood.

   EXEMPLE   — **Brigitte était de très bonne humeur.**
                       — **Peut-être qu'elle a eu 20 à son interro de maths.**

   MA PHOTO :

2. Now you're curious about the party your partner attended. Listen as your partner describes how each guest was feeling. After each of your partner's descriptions, write the person's name and tell your partner why you think the person felt that way. Write your explanation in the space provided. When you've finished, compare papers to see if you have the correct names.

   LA PHOTO DE MON/MA CAMARADE :

   Nom   **Raison**

   1. _____   _____

   2. _____   _____

   3. _____   _____

   4. _____   _____

Communicative Activity 9-1B

1. Situation   Your partner went to a party last weekend, and you want to hear all about it.

Task   Listen as your partner describes how each guest was feeling. After each of your partner's descriptions, write the person's name and tell your partner why you think the person felt that way. Write your explanation in the space provided.

EXEMPLE   — **Brigitte était de très bonne humeur.**
                 — **Peut-être qu'elle a eu 20 à son interro de maths.**

LA PHOTO DE MON/MA CAMARADE :

	Nom	**Raison**
1.	_____	_____
2.	_____	_____
3.	_____	_____
4.	_____	_____

2. Now your partner is curious about the party you attended. Look at the group photo below and tell your partner how each guest was feeling. After each description, your partner will offer a possible explanation for the person's mood. When you've finished, compare papers to see if you have the correct names.

MA PHOTO :

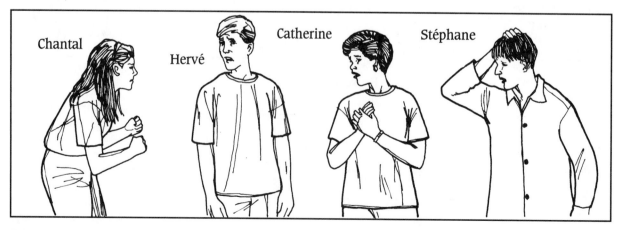

Chantal   Hervé   Catherine   Stéphane

French 2 Allez, viens!, Chapter 9

1. Situation A UFO has landed in your town! You and your partner are newspaper reporters. You've just finished asking different people what they were doing when the UFO landed.

Task Ask your partner what the people listed below were doing. Then write their names under the appropriate pictures according to your partner's answers.

EXEMPLE — Qu'est-ce qu'elle faisait, Mme Lebrun?
— Elle promenait le chien.

LES PERSONNES QUE MON/MA CAMARADE A INTERVIEWEES :

 Mme Lebrun   Siméon   M. Garnier   les Ripoche   Joëlle

_____ _____ _____

_____ _____

2. Now answer your partner's questions about the people pictured below. When you've finished, compare papers to make sure you have the correct names.

LES PERSONNES QUE J'AI INTERVIEWEES :

M. Prévost   Eric et Sylvie   Didier

Fatima   Marc et Christelle

Nom_____ Classe_____ Date_____

Communicative Activity 9-2B

1. Situation A UFO has landed in your town! You and your partner are newspaper reporters. You've just finished asking different people what they were doing when the UFO landed.

Task Tell your partner what the people pictured below were doing.

LES PERSONNES QUE J'AI INTERVIEWEES :

Mme Lebrun

Joëlle

les Ripoche

Siméon

M. Garnier

2. Now ask your partner what the people listed below were doing. Then write their names under the appropriate pictures according to your partner's answer. When you've finished, compare papers to make sure you have the correct names.

EXEMPLE   — Qu'est-ce qu'il faisait, M. Prévost?
               — Il lisait le journal.

LES PERSONNES QUE MON/MA CAMARADE A INTERVIEWEES :

M. Prévost   Fatima   Marc et Christelle   Didier   Eric et Sylvie

Nom_____ Classe_____ Date_____

1. **Situation** You and your partner are making a movie. Each of you has created sketches of the various important scenes that will be in your film. Now you're going over the story and the sketches together.

   Task Begin telling the story based on the first drawing in the sequence below. Your partner will continue the story based on his or her drawing. Write down the scene he or she describes in the space provided, then tell what happened next based on the next drawing on your page. Continue taking turns until you and your partner have described each scene of the story.

   EXEMPLE — **Monsieur Ducerf était très fatigué...**

1.

2. _____
   _____
   _____
   _____
   _____
   _____

3.

4. _____
   _____
   _____
   _____
   _____
   _____

5.

6. _____
   _____
   _____
   _____
   _____
   _____

2. Now decide together what the final scene of your movie will be like. Draw a sketch of it in the box below and describe what happened in the space provided.

   _____
   _____
   _____
   _____
   _____
   _____
   _____
   _____
   _____

French 2 Allez, viens!, Chapter 9

Activities for Communication **53**

Communicative Activity 9-3B

1. Situation   You and your partner are making a movie. Each of you has created sketches of the various important scenes that will be in your film. Now you're going over the story and the sketches together.

Task   Your partner will begin telling the story. Write down the scene he or she describes in the space provided. Then continue the story based on the first drawing on your page. Your partner will write down the scene you describe and then tell what happened next. Continue taking turns until you and your partner have described each scene of the story.

EXEMPLE   — Monsieur Ducerf était très fatigué...

1. _____

_____

_____

_____

_____

2.

3. _____

_____

_____

_____

_____

4.

5. _____

_____

_____

_____

6.

2. Now decide together what the final scene of your movie will be like. Draw a sketch of it in the box below and describe what happened in the space provided.

_____

_____

_____

_____

_____

_____

_____

_____

1. Situation   You would like your partner's advice about some problems you're having.

Task   Explain each situation to your partner based on the suggestions listed below. Then write down your partner's advice.

EXEMPLE — J'ai un problème. J'ai oublié l'anniversaire de ma mère. A ton avis, qu'est-ce que je dois faire?
— Explique-lui que...

1. oublier l'anniversaire de ma mère _____

_____

2. perdre les CD de ma sœur _____

_____

3. casser l'appareil-photo de mon père _____

_____

4. rater l'examen de sciences nat _____

_____

5. casser avec mon copain/ma copine _____

_____

2. Change roles. Now your partner will tell you about some problems he or she is having. Offer advice using expressions from the word box below. Try to use each expression only once.

> Dis-lui que...   Invite-le/-la...   Téléphone-lui.
>
> Tu devrais...   Oublie-le/-la/-les.
>
> Excuse-toi.   Parle-lui.   Explique-lui que...

COMMUNICATIVE ACTIVITIES

Communicative Activity 10-1B

1. **Situation**   Your partner would like your advice about some problems he or she is having.

   Task   Your partner will tell you about some problems he or she is having. Offer advice using expressions from the word box below. Try to use each expression only once.

   EXEMPLE   — J'ai un problème. J'ai oublié l'anniversaire de ma mère. A ton avis, qu'est-ce que je dois faire?
                      — Explique-lui que...

   > Dis-lui que...   Invite-le/-la...   Téléphone-lui.
   >
   > Tu devrais...   Oublie-le/-la/-les.
   >
   > Excuse-toi.   Parle-lui.   Explique-lui que...

2. Change roles. Now you want your partner's advice for some problems you're having. Explain each situation to your partner, based on the suggestions below. Then write down your partner's advice.

   1. marcher sur les plantes dans le jardin de ma tante _____

   _____

   2. me disputer avec mon ami(e) _____

   _____

   3. rater un rendez-vous avec mon copain/ma copine _____

   _____

   4. oublier mes devoirs de biologie à la maison _____

   _____

   5. avoir de mauvaises notes dans mon bulletin trimestriel _____

   _____

Nom_____ Classe_____ Date_____

1. **Situation** You need some help preparing a party.

Task Ask your partner to do each of the tasks pictured below. Place a check mark under the tasks your partner agrees to do for you and an X under those he or she refuses to do.

EXEMPLE — **Tu pourrais faire le ménage?**
— **Bien sûr.**
or
— **Désolé(e), je n'ai pas le temps.**

MES TACHES MENAGERES :

2. Now your partner has some favors to ask of you. Listen as he or she asks you to do the tasks pictured below. Agree to do the task if it's marked with a check mark; refuse to do the task and make an excuse if it's marked with an X. When you've finished, compare papers to make sure they match.

LES TACHES MENAGERES DE MON/MA CAMARADE :

 ✔    ✗

 ✔    ✗

Communicative Activity 10-2B

1. Situation Your partner would like your help with preparing a party.

Task Listen as he or she asks you to do the tasks pictured below. Agree to do the task if it's marked with a check mark; refuse to do the task and make an excuse if it's marked with an X.

LES TACHES MENAGERES DE MON/MA CAMARADE :

✓

X

X

✓

2. Now you have some favors to ask of your partner. Ask him or her to do each of the tasks pictured below. Place a check mark under the tasks your partner agrees to do for you and an X under those he or she refuses to do. When you've finished, compare papers to make sure they match.

EXEMPLE — **Tu pourrais demander la permission à tes parents?**
— **Bien sûr.**
or
— **Non, c'est impossible.**

MES TACHES MENAGERES :

_____

_____

_____

_____

French 2 Allez, viens!, Chapter 10

1. Situation   Your partner recently cleaned out his or her closet and gave away certain items to friends. But you think the items should have gone to family members.

Task   Ask your partner to whom he or she gave each of the items pictured below. Then tell your partner to whom he or she should or could have given the item, choosing a family member from the box.

EXEMPLE
— Qu'est-ce que tu as fait de ton pull?
— Je l'ai donné à Mireille.
— Tu aurais dû/aurais pu...

1. 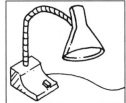   2.    3.

4.    5.    6.

ton cousin
ton oncle
ton grand-père
ta cousine
ta sœur
ton frère

2. You also cleaned out your closet. But you gave certain items away to family members. Your partner thinks you should have given them to your friends. Tell him or her to whom you gave each item.

1.

ma sœur

2.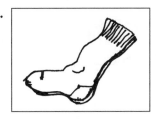

mon frère

3.

ma tante

4.

mon grand-père

5.

mon cousin

6.

ma cousine

COMMUNICATIVE ACTIVITIES

Communicative Activity 10-3B

1. Situation   You recently cleaned out your closet and gave certain items away to friends. Your partner thinks you should have given the items to family members.

Task   Tell your partner to whom you gave each item pictured below.

1.

   Ahmed

2.

   Mireille

3.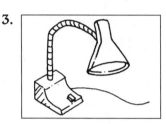

   Li

4.

   Prisca

5.

   Etienne

6.

   Rémy

2. Your partner also recently cleaned out his or her closet and gave away certain items to family members. But you think the items should have gone to friends. Ask your partner to whom he or she gave each of the items pictured below. Then tell your partner to whom he or she should or could have given the item, choosing a friend's name from the word box.

EXEMPLE   — Qu'est-ce que tu as fait de ton manteau?
                         — Je l'ai donné à ma sœur.
                         — Tu aurais dû/aurais pu...

1.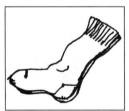

2.

3.

4.

5.

6.

Mireille
Etienne
Rémy
Prisca
Ahmed
Li

French 2 Allez, viens!, Chapter 10

1. **Situation**   Your French pen pal has sent you a list of musicians so that you can become familiar with different types of music from French-speaking countries. When you go to the music store you realize that you don't know what type of music the different artists perform. You seek the help of a store employee (your partner).

Task   Ask your partner if he or she has heard of each musician on your list. Then fill in the information next to each artist's name.

EXEMPLE   — Est-ce que vous connaissez... ?
                    — Bien sûr, c'est un(e)...

1. Isabelle Boulay _____

2. Claude Debussy _____

3. Sonia Dersion _____

4. Les Innocents _____

5. Alain Bashung _____

2. Change roles. Now you're the music store employee and your partner has a list of musicians he or she needs help with. When your partner asks about a musician on his or her list, tell who the musician is and describe his or her music.

artiste	profil	musique
1. Rachid Taha	chanteur algérien-français	raï/chansons arabes
2. Jacques Brel	chanteur belge	chansons classiques françaises
3. MC Solaar	chanteur français	rap
4. Patricia Kaas	chanteuse française	pop
5. Amadou & Mariam	groupe africain	blues africain

Now, based on the information from both lists above, tell your partner which CDs you would like to buy and why.

J'aimerais acheter...

Communicative Activity 11-1B

1. **Situation** You're an employee at a music store that sells music from around the world. Your partner needs help with a list of musicians from French-speaking countries.

Task When your partner asks about a musician on his or her list, tell who the musician is and describe his or her music.

EXEMPLE — Est-ce que vous connaissez... ?
— Bien sûr, c'est un(e)...

artiste	profil	musique
1. Isabelle Boulay	chanteuse canadienne	pop/folk
2. Claude Debussy	compositeur français	classique
3. Sonia Dersion	chanteuse antillaise	zouk
4. Les Innocents	groupe français	pop/rock
5. Alain Bashung	chanteur français	rock

2. Change roles. Now you're looking for music that was suggested to you by a French-speaking pen pal. Your partner is an employee at a music store. Ask your partner if he or she has heard of each of the artists on your list. Then fill in the information next to each artist's name.

1. Rachid Taha _____

2. Jacques Brel _____

3. MC Solaar _____

4. Patricia Kaas _____

5. Amadou & Mariam _____

Now, based on the information from both lists above, tell your partner which CDs you would like to buy and why.

J'aimerais acheter...

Communicative Activity 11-2A

Situation   You and your partner work at a movie theater. You've been asked to change films on the marquee, but you don't have all the necessary information.

Task   First ask your partner for the information you're missing. Then answer your partner's questions about the information he or she is missing. Take turns. When you've finished, compare papers to make sure you have the same information.

EXEMPLE
— Le film *Aladdin,* c'est avec qui?
— C'est avec Robin Williams.
— C'est quel genre?
— C'est un film...
— Ça commence à quelle heure?
— ...

LES RENSEIGNEMENTS QU'IL ME FAUT :

CINE MULTIPLEX

Salle 1   *Aladdin*

_____

_____

_____

Salle 2   _____

Gary Oldman, Anthony Hopkins

_____

_____

Salle 3   _____

_____

19h30

Salle 4   *Titanic*

_____

_____

LES RENSEIGNEMENTS POUR MON/MA CAMARADE :

CINE MULTIPLEX

Salle 5   *Cyrano de Bergerac*

Gérard Depardieu, Anne Brochet

film classique

18h15

Salle 6   *La Belle et la Bête*

Jean Marais

film d'amour

12h20

Salle 7   *Star Trek 5: L'Ultime Frontière*

Willliam Shatner, Leonard Nemoy

film de science-fiction

11h05

Salle 8   *Les Trois Mousquetaires*

Keifer Sutherland

film d'aventures

21h00

Communicative Activity 11-2B

Situation   You and your partner work at a movie theater. You've been asked to change the films on the marquee, but you don't have all the necessary information.

Task   First answer your partner's question about the information he or she is missing. Then ask your partner for the information you're missing. Take turns. When you've finished, compare papers to make sure you have the same information.

EXEMPLE — Le film *Aladdin,* c'est avec qui?
— C'est avec Robin Williams.
— C'est quel genre?
— C'est un film...
— Ça commence à quelle heure?
— ...

LES RENSEIGNEMENTS POUR MON/MA CAMARADE :

```
                         CINE MULTIPLEX
```

Salle 1   *Aladdin*   **Salle 3**   *Demain ne meurt jamais*

   Robin Williams   Pierce Brosnan

   film comique   film d'action

   13h30   19h30

Salle 2   *Dracula*   **Salle 4**   *Titanic*

   Gary Oldman, Anthony Hopkins   Leonardo DiCaprio, Kate Winslet

   film d'horreur   film d'aventures

   14h10   20h45

LES RENSEIGNEMENTS QU'IL ME FAUT :

```
                         CINE MULTIPLEX
```

Salle 5   _____   **Salle 7**   *Star Trek 5: L'Ultime Frontière*

   Gérard Depardieu, Anne Brochet   _____

   _____   _____

   _____

Salle 6   _____   **Salle 8**   _____

   _____   Keifer Sutherland

   _____   _____

   12h20   _____

French 2 Allez, viens!, Chapter 11

Situation   You and your partner are trying to decide what to buy in a bookstore. You have the book review section of one newspaper, and your partner has the reviews from a different newspaper.

Task   Ask your partner what the critic for his or her newspaper, Monsieur Lefranc, has to say about the books on your list. Then answer your partner's questions about the reviews of Mademoiselle Lesage, the critic in your newspaper. Take turns. When you've finished, compare your papers to find out which books the critics both liked or didn't like. Which books are you going to buy, based on their recommendations?

EXEMPLE   — Qu'est-ce qu'il dit du *Comte de Monte-Cristo*, **Monsieur Lefranc?**
                 — Il dit qu'on ne s'ennuie pas.

LES OPINIONS DE M. LEFRANC :

Roman	Opinion
Le Comte de Monte-Cristo	
Les Trois Mousquetaires	
Les Misérables	
L'Etranger	
Le Misanthrope	
L'Enfant noir	
La Princesse de Clèves	

LES OPINIONS DE MLLE LESAGE :

Roman	Opinion
Le Comte de Monte-Cristo	C'est un roman d'aventures classique.
Les Trois Mousquetaires	C'est une belle histoire.
Les Misérables	C'est bête.
L'Etranger	Il n'y a pas d'histoire.
Le Misanthrope	C'est amusant.
L'Enfant noir	C'est une belle histoire.
La Princesse de Clèves	C'est du n'importe quoi.

Communicative Activity 11-3B

Situation You and your partner are trying to decide what to buy in a bookstore. You have the book review section of one newspaper, and your partner has the reviews from a different newspaper.

Task Answer your partner's questions about the reviews of Monsieur Lefranc, the critic in your newspaper. Then ask your partner what the critic for his or her paper, Mademoiselle Lesage, has to say about the books on your list and write down her remarks. Take turns. When you've finished, compare your papers to find out which books the critics both liked or didn't like. Which books are you going to buy, based on their recommendations?

EXEMPLE — Qu'est-ce qu'il dit du *Comte de Monte-Cristo,* **Monsieur Lefranc?**
— Il dit qu'on ne s'ennuie pas.

LES OPINIONS DE M. LEFRANC :

Roman	Opinion
Le Comte de Monte-Cristo	On ne s'ennuie pas.
Les Trois Mousquetaires	C'est trop long.
Les Misérables	C'est une histoire passionnante.
L'Etranger	C'est déprimant.
Le Misanthrope	C'est une pièce comique et classique.
L'Enfant noir	C'est une histoire passionnante.
La Princesse de Clèves	C'est plein de rebondissements.

LES OPINIONS DE MLLE LESAGE :

Roman	Opinion
Le Comte de Monte-Cristo	
Les Trois Mousquetaires	
Les Misérables	
L'Etranger	
Le Misanthrope	
L'Enfant noir	
La Princesse de Clèves	

Communicative Activity 12-1A ✳

1. **Situation**   You're a travel agent trying to arrange wilderness vacations for several clients. You telephone an employee of the national park service (your partner) to ask what activities are available at the parks listed in the chart below.

   Task   Check the activities that are available in each park. Then look at the activities your clients want to do and write down the name of the park that would best suit each person.

   EXEMPLE   — Qu'est-ce qu'il y a à faire au parc du Mont-Tremblant?
                        — On peut faire...

   LES PARCS :

Nom du parc	🏕	🛷	🚴	🤾	🪑	🛶	🚶	⛵
Mont-Tremblant								
Jacques-Cartier								
Mont-Saint-Bruno								
Yamaska								
Mont-Orford								
Frontenac								

   MES CLIENTS :

   Mme Boyer   🏕 🛷 🪑   _____

   Mlle Nortier   🚶 ⛵ 🛷   _____

   M. Muboto   🛶 🚴 🏕   _____

2. Now answer your partner's questions about the activities available at the parks listed in the chart below. When you've finished, compare papers to make sure you have the correct information.

   LES PARCS :

Nom du parc	🏕	🛷	🚴	🤾	🪑	🛶	🚶	⛵
Grands-Jardins	✓	✓			✓	✓		
Pointe-Taillon				✓	✓		✓	
Saguenay	✓		✓		✓	✓		✓
Bic		✓			✓		✓	✓
Gaspésie				✓		✓	✓	
Ile Bonaventure	✓	✓	✓					✓

Communicative Activity 12-1B

1. **Situation** You're an employee of the national park service. Your partner, a travel agent, calls you to inquire about the activities available at the parks listed in the chart below.

   Task Answer his or her questions.

   EXEMPLE — Qu'est-ce qu'il y a à faire au parc du Mont-Tremblant?
   — On peut faire...

LES PARCS :

Nom du parc	⛺	🏍	🚲	⛷	⛱	🛷	🚶	⛵
Mont-Tremblant		✓	✓				✓	✓
Jacques-Cartier			✓			✓		✓
Mont-Saint-Bruno	✓			✓			✓	
Yamaska	✓	✓			✓			✓
Mont-Orford	✓		✓			✓		
Frontenac	✓			✓	✓			

2. Now you're trying to arrange wilderness vacations for several clients. You telephone an employee of the national park service (your partner) to ask what activities are available at the parks listed in the chart below. Check the activities that are available in each park. Then look at the activities your clients want to do and write down the name of the park that would best suit each person. When you've finished, compare papers to make sure you have the correct information.

LES PARCS :

Nom du parc	⛺	🏍	🚲	⛷	⛱	🛷	🚶	⛵
Grands-Jardins								
Pointe-Taillon								
Saguenay								
Bic								
Gaspésie								
Ile Bonaventure								

MES CLIENTS :

Mme Ducharme _____

Mlle Champeny _____

M. Prévost _____

1. Situation   You and your partner are about to take a camping trip in the mountains. You've never been to the mountains before and you want to know what to pack. Your partner has been camping in the mountains several times before.

Task   Ask your partner what you should take on your trip to the mountains. Check off each item he or she mentions that is already on your list. Write down any items that you need to add in the space provided.

EXEMPLE   — **Qu'est-ce que je dois emporter pour faire du camping en montagne?**
                   — **Tu ferais bien d'emporter...**

MA LISTE :

     1. une canne à pêche
     2. un sac de couchage
     3. des chaussures de randonnée
     4. une bouteille d'eau
     5. une lampe de poche

Il faut aussi...

_____

_____

_____

2. Now you and your partner are going camping at the beach. Your partner has never been camping at the beach before, but you've been several times. Advise your partner what he or she should should take on the trip, based on the items shown below.

Now compare papers with your partner to be sure you both have the same information.

Communicative Activity 12-2B

1. Situation   You and your partner are about to take a camping trip in the mountains. Your partner has never been to the mountains before, but you've been several times.

Task   Advise your partner what he or she should take on the trip, based on the items shown below.

EXEMPLE   — Qu'est-ce que je dois emporter pour faire du camping en montagne?
               — Tu ferais bien d'emporter...

2. Now you and your partner are going camping at the beach. You've never been camping at the beach before, but your partner has been several times. Ask your partner what you should take on the trip. Check off each item that is already on your list. Write down any items you need to add in the space provided.

MA LISTE :

1. un maillot de bain
2. des sandales
3. des allumettes
4. une tente
5. un sac de couchage

Il faut aussi...

_____

_____

_____

Now compare papers with your partner to be sure you both have the same information.

1. Situation   Your partner has just returned from a nature walk.

Task   Using sequencing words, ask your partner to describe what he or she saw. Draw the items as he or she describes them.

EXEMPLE   — Qu'est-ce que tu as vu d'abord?
                     — D'abord, j'ai vu...
                     — Et ensuite?

LA RANDONNEE DE MON/MA CAMARADE :

2. Now use the map below to answer your partner's questions about what you saw on your nature walk. Imagine that your walk began on the left side of the page and ended on the right. When you've finished, compare papers to make sure you have the same information.

MA RANDONNEE :

Communicative Activity 12-3B

1. **Situation**   You've just returned from a nature walk. Your partner wants to know what you saw.

   Task   Use the map below to answer his or her questions. Imagine that your walk began on the left side of the page and ended on the right.

   EXEMPLE   — Qu'est-ce que tu as vu d'abord?
                    — D'abord, j'ai vu...
                    — Et ensuite?

MA RANDONNEE :

2. Now, using sequencing words, ask what your partner saw on his or her nature walk. Draw the items he or she saw along the way. When you've finished, compare papers to make sure you have the same information.

LA RANDONNEE DE MON/MA CAMARADE :

French 2 Allez, viens!, Chapter 12

Realia and Suggestions
for Using Realia

Cédric. 18 ans. Habite Aix-en-Provence, dans les Bouches-du-Rhône. En première année d'histoire de l'art à l'université. A déjà travaillé dans une galerie d'art. Veut être conservateur de musée. Mère artiste, père artisan.

Pascale. 17 ans. Habite Aix-en-Provence, dans les Bouches-du-Rhône. En première. A travaillé comme animatrice de colonies de vacances et comme accompagnatrice pour des voyages scolaires. Veut aller faire ses études à Berlin et y travailler comme professeur de français. Mère sans profession, père responsable administratif.

Stéphane. 17 ans. Habite à Fort-de-France, en Martinique. En terminale. A travaillé comme serveur dans un restaurant. Veut entrer aux Beaux-Arts après son bac. Ne sait pas quelle profession il veut exercer. Mère infirmière, père pompier.

Sandrine. 16 ans. Habite à Abidjan, en Côte d'Ivoire. En seconde au lycée Houphouët-Boigny. Parle français, anglais et espagnol. Veut faire des études de sciences politiques. Voudrait devenir diplomate. Père pilote, mère marchande.

Fabien. 16 ans. Habite à Biarritz, dans les Pyrénées-Atlantiques. En seconde. Veut faire des études de mathématiques ou de sciences. N'est pas encore certain de ce qu'il veut faire plus tard, peut-être ingénieur. Mère professeur de français, père informaticien.

Irène. 17 ans. Habite à Dijon, dans la Côte-d'Or. Travaille comme apprentie dans un salon de coiffure depuis six mois. Veut ouvrir son propre salon. Mère institutrice, père commerçant.

Léonard. 19 ans. Habite à Toulouse, dans la Haute-Garonne. En prépa médecine vétérinaire. Travaille comme volontaire à la Société de protection des animaux de Toulouse. Veut être vétérinaire. Mère avocate, père professeur de sport.

Mathilde. 17 ans. Habite à Pointe-à-Pitre, en Guadeloupe. En première, section arts. Veut faire une école de stylisme de mode. A déjà travaillé comme vendeuse dans un magasin de vêtements. Veut devenir styliste de mode. Parents restaurateurs.

REALIA

Realia 1-2

FRANCE METEOROLOGIE

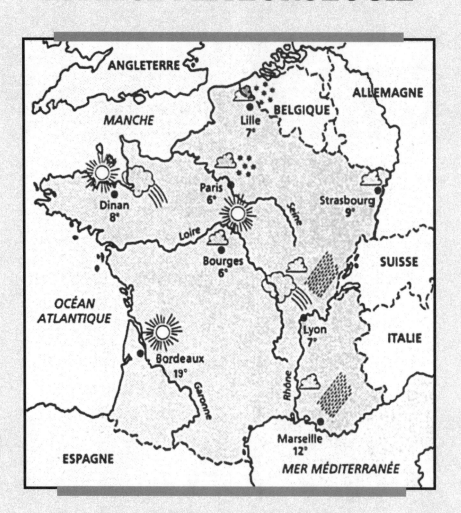

ANGLETERRE

ALLEMAGNE

MANCHE

BELGIQUE

Lille
7°

Dinan
8°

Paris
6°

Strasbourg
9°

Loire

Bourges
6°

SUISSE

OCÉAN
ATLANTIQUE

Lyon
7°

ITALIE

Bordeaux
19°

Garonne

Rhône

ESPAGNE

Marseille
12°

MER MÉDITERRANÉE

Températures Mondiales

Londres	6		Abidjan	27
Berlin	4		Dakar	23
Genève	6		Beirut	14
Bruxelles	3		Hanoi	13
Madrid	10		New York	-6
Rome	15		Montréal	-6
Moscou	-5		Lima	21
Casablanca	18		Fort-de-France	26

Paris → Dijon → Lausanne / Bern et Zurich

PRIX

1	3	Pour connaître le prix de votre billet, consultez :
2		-Si vous voyagez en 1ʳᵉ classe la page 50
		-Si vous voyagez en 2ᵉ classe la page 51

HORAIRES

N° du TGV		EC 21	EC 23	EC 25	EC 29	EC 429	EC 27
Restauration		▣	▣		▣	▣	▣
Paris-Gare de Lyon	D	7.18	12.41	15.48	16.52	16.52	17.52
Dijon	A	8.58	14.21	17.28	18.34	18.34	19.34
Dole	A	9.24					
Mouchard	A	9.46					20.17
Frasne	A	10.24	15.37	18.45	19.52	19.52	20.54
Vallorbe	A	10.44	15.56	19.04	20.13		21.13
Lausanne	A	11.18	16.30	19.38	20.47		21.47
Pontarlier	A	a 10.41				20.06	a 21.19
Neuchâtel	A	a 11.24				20.49	a 22.04
Biel/Bienne	A	a 11.45					a 22.25
Bern	A	a 12.13	b	b	b	21.22	a 22.53
Olten	A					22.10	
Aarau	A					22.20	
Zurich	A					22.47	

SEMAINES TYPES

du 24 mai	Lundi	3	2		1	1	2
au 12 juillet	Mardi à Jeudi	3	1		1	1	3
et du 31 août	Vendredi	3	1	3		3	3
au 28 novembre	Samedi	2	2		1	1	2
	Dimanche	1	1	3		3	3
du 13 juillet	Lundi	1	2		1	1	2
au 30 août	Mardi à Jeudi	1	2		1	1	2
	Vendredi	1	2	3		3	3
	Samedi	1	2		2	2	2
	Dimanche	1	1	3		3	2

JOURS PARTICULIERS

Mai	Dimanche 24	1	3	3		3	3
	Dimanche 31	1	1		1	1	1
Juin	Lundi 1ᵉʳ	1	3	3		3	3
	Mardi 2	3	2		1	1	2
Juillet	Dimanche 12	1	1			1	1
	Lundi 13	1	2		1	1	1
	Mardi 14	1	1	3		3	2
Septembre	Lundi 21	3	2		3	3	3

D   Départ   A Arrivée
EC   TGV Eurocity
a   Correspondance à Frasne.
b   Correspondance à Lausanne.
▣   Service restauration à la place en 1ʳᵉ classe, en réservation.

REALIA

Excerpts from *Guide TGV Sud-Est,* May 24–November 28, 1998, by SNCF. Reprinted by permission of ***SNCF: Direction Grandes Lignes.***

Using Realia: Chapter 1

Using Realia 1-1: Personal profiles

1. **Reading:** Have students find the types or categories of information provided in each biography. Have them make a chart showing each person's name, age, hometown, schooling, work experience, career plans, and parents' occupations.

2. **Listening:** Read aloud statements several of the people might make. (**J'ai 17 ans. Je veux être professeur.**) Have students indicate which person is speaking.

3. **Speaking:** Have students work in pairs. One student plays the role of one of the young people from the profiles. The other student interviews him or her, making up questions based on the information in the profile. Have partners change roles.

4. **Writing:** Have students write a personal profile of themselves, of a friend, or of a famous or imaginary person.

5. **Culture:** Tell students that students in France begin to choose a major field of study when they are fourteen or fifteen years old. French students take a series of tests to determine their aptitude in the field of study they wish to pursue. Have students research the French school system or provide them with information found in Culture Notes from the *Allez, viens! Annotated Teacher's Edition, Level 2*, p. 128 and p. 135. Have students choose a field of study and write out what their curriculum might be if they were students in a French high school. You may want to provide a list of the school subjects in French as a review for the students.

6. **Culture:** Remind students that French high school students usually take two foreign language courses. Notice how many languages Sandrine speaks. Read aloud the Culture Note about High School in Côte d'Ivoire found in the *Allez, viens! Annotated Teacher's Edition, Level 2*, p. 228. Ask students why there might be more emphasis on foreign languages in the French school system than in American schools. Students may refer to the map of the Francophone World on p. xxv to see which countries border Côte d'Ivoire and whether or not they are French-speaking countries.

Using Realia 1-2: Weather map

1. **Listening:** Distribute copies of the weather map. Describe the weather in one of the French cities shown on the map. (**Il fait du soleil, mais il fait très froid.**) Then have students circle the city or cities on the map where the weather icons match the weather you have described. You might show a transparency of the map as you do the activity and have students check their answers against yours after each weather description.

2. **Reading:** Distribute copies of the weather map to students. Have them use colored pencils or pens to indicate on the map the different bodies of water and country boundaries. Have students create a list of French-speaking and non-French-speaking cities from the list below the map.

3. **Speaking:** Have students work in small groups. One student tells where he or she plans to go on vacation based on the locations shown on the weather map. The other students take turns advising what he or she should take on the trip. Students should change roles until each person in the group has told where he or she wants to go on vacation.

4. **Writing:** Have students imagine that a French pen pal is coming to visit. Students should write a short letter to their pen pal telling what the weather is like in their town and what items their pen pal should bring on the trip.

5. **Culture:** Remind students of the difference between Fahrenheit and Celsius. (To convert Fahrenheit to Celsius, subtract 32 and then multiply by 5/9.) Have students determine what season or month it might be, according to how cold or warm the temperatures are.

6. **Culture:** Have students research the name of the country where each of the cities listed below the weather map is located. Then ask them to name which of these are French-speaking countries. You might provide students with a blank map of the world and have them mark the appropriate countries and cities and color code those that are French-speaking.

Using Realia 1-3: Train schedule

1. **Reading:** Distribute copies of the train schedule to students. Point out that the symbols on the schedule are explained in the legend and remind students that official times in France are given with a 24-hour clock. After students have had a chance to get familiar with the schedule, have them answer the following questions about travel from Paris to Lausanne or Bern: How many times a week can you travel from Paris to Lausanne? Which days? How long does the trip take? What sort of amenities are provided for the passengers?

2. **Listening:** After students are familiar with the layout of the schedule, read aloud a series of sentences telling at what time you are leaving from Paris and at what time you will arrive at your destination. Then have students name the train you are taking.

3. **Speaking:** Have students work in pairs to discuss a trip from Paris to one of the cities listed on the train schedule. One student should suggest a trip, giving the time and day of the departure. The other should accept or refuse the invitation and explain why.

4. **Speaking:** Have students work in pairs to plan for an upcoming trip to Lausanne. First they should determine when they will leave based on the information from the train schedule. Then students should make a list of the things they need to do before going and explain what they will do first, next, and so on.

5. **Writing:** Have students work in groups to create a schedule that shows trains returning to Paris from Lausanne or Bern. Ask students to include a legend for any symbols they choose to include on their schedule.

Realia 2-1

Avez-vous beaucoup de savoir-vivre?

A. Quand vous êtes invité chez des amis à dîner...

1. Vous demandez à l'hôte de changer la date du dîner parce que vous êtes occupé le soir où il vous a invité.

2. Vous offrez d'apporter quelque chose, par exemple un dessert.

3. Vous apportez des fleurs.

4. Vous demandez qui sont les autres invités parce que vous n'aimez pas tous les amis de l'hôte. Vous suggérez d'autres personnes à inviter.

B. Vous n'aimez pas du tout le plat principal que l'hôte a préparé...

1. Vous êtes franc et vous dites que vous détestez ce plat.

2. Vous mangez tout et quand l'hôte vous demande si c'était bon, vous répondez «Oui, c'était excellent.»

3. Vous expliquez à l'hôte que vous ne pouvez pas en prendre parce que vous êtes allergique à certains aliments.

4. Vous essayez d'avaler quelques morceaux et vous faites le dégoûté avec le reste. L'hôte vous demande si vous n'aimez pas le plat et vous répondez que vous n'avez pas faim.

C. Quand vous recevez des amis chez vous...

1. Vous leur dites «Faites comme chez vous.»

2. Vous n'êtes pas encore prêt. Vous dites à vos amis qu'ils peuvent regarder la télévision ou écouter de la musique, mais vous oubliez de leur offrir des amuse-gueule.

3. Vous leur offrez quelque chose à boire ou à manger.

4. Vous êtes tous à table quand vous recevez un coup de téléphone d'un ami cher qui vit à l'étranger.

　　a. Vous lui dites que vous avez des invités et que vous le rappellerez plus tard.

　　b. Vous faites des excuses à vos invités et vous parlez avec votre ami pendant vingt minutes.

French 2 Allez, viens!, Chapter 2

APPARTEMENTS

Le Triplex

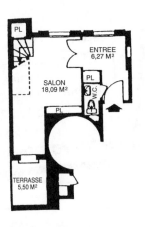

niveau inférieur

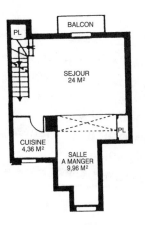

niveau moyen

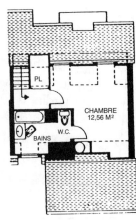

niveau supérieur

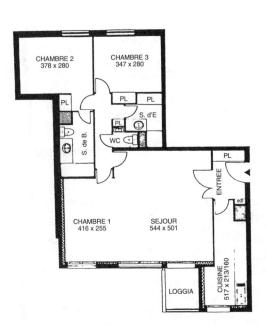

Appartement 1

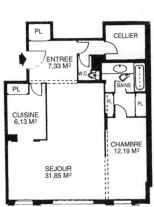

Appartement 2

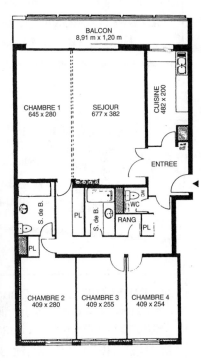

Appartement 3

R E A L I A

Realia 2-3

MAISONS LOIRE ATLANTIQUE

REZE, proche Sèvre. Agréable maison des années 50, rénovée. Séj./salon sur jardin, 3 chbres, petit bureau. Garage. **115 860 €.**
GADEL BAZIN IMMOBILIER – Nantes
Tél. 02.40.80.04.35

HAUTE GOULAINE. Maison spacieuse de 5 chbres dont 3 en RDC. 2 sdb, salon/séj. cheminée, cuis. équipée, lingerie, Garage/2 voitures. Terrain arboré 1500m2 sans vis-à-vis.
154 430 €. FAI
JEFIMMO – Thouaré – Tél. 02.40.68.04.20

HAUTE GOULAINE. Agréable maison tradit. Séjour cheminée 35m2, 5 chbres, cuisine, lingerie, salle de jeux. Cellier, garage. Terrain. Belle affaire. **125 000 €.**
BEAUPERE-MONNIER IMMOBILIER
Rezé – Tél. 02.40.75.68.72

10mn Sud/Ouest. Le charme des années 30. Séj./salon 56m2 très lumineux, 4 chbres, bureau. Piscine. Terrain 1700m2. **A voir. 211 140 €.**
GADEL BAZIN IMMOBILIER – Nantes
Tél. 02.40.80.04.35

BOUGUENAIS. Architecture contemporaine. Beau séj./salon, 4 chbres, 2 bains. Garage. Jardin. **130 340 €.**
GADEL BAZIN IMMOBILIER – Nantes
Tél. 02.40.80.04.35

LA BAULE face mer, entre casino et centre ville. Etat impec. Gd studio 41m2, cuisine éq., bains, wc, lingerie. **67 100 €.**
Ph. CONAN-OUEST UNION – La Baule
Tél. 02.40.24.12.61

SUD LOIRE. 120m2 superbe séj. cheminée, 4 chbres. Jardin. Terrasse. Proche commerces et bus. **135 700 €.**
MOREL-HENRY IMMOBILIER – Nantes
Tél. 02.40.20.16.00

LA BAULE Centre. Dans petit collectif de grand standing, face mer. A saisir. Appt de 91m2 face à la mer. Terrasse 30m2. Jardin privatif 130m2. Entrée, dressing, cuis. équipée, salon/séj. 30m2, 2 chbres, 2 sdb.
REF. GR559 340 000 €. CC
AGIPORT IMMOBILIER – Pornichet
Tél. 02.40.61.18.50

Adaptation of real estate advertisements from pages 6 and 8 of "FNAIM Loire Atlantique" from *Le Magazine de l'Immoblier 44: FNAIM,* no. 4. Reprinted by permission of *FNAIM.*

Using Realia 2-1: Questionnaire on manners

1. **Listening:** Read various sentences from the questionnaire aloud to the class. For each of the phrases you read, have students guess if it is something the guest would say or do, or something the host would say or do. For example, the host might say, **Faites comme chez vous,** and the guest might say, **Je vous ai apporté des fleurs.**

2. **Reading:** Have students read the questionnaire, and then tell which responses they think are polite and which they think are impolite.

3. **Reading:** Have the students read the questionnaire and select the response which they think they would be most likely to say or do in each of the situations.

4. **Speaking:** Have the students pair off and pretend that they are having a dinner party. One student will act as the host and the other will act as the guest. Students should act out one scenario for each of the situations presented in the questionnaire.

5. **Writing:** Have students write a conversation in French between a host and a guest. The host should try to make the guest feel more comfortable and the guest should respond appropriately.

6. **Culture:** Tell students that in France it is common and polite for the guest to bring flowers or some sort of gift when they are invited to someone's house. Ask students if this courtesy or a similar polite gesture is found in their own culture.

Using Realia 2-2: Apartment floor plans

1. **Listening:** You're a real estate agent describing one of the apartments. Have students try to guess which apartment you're talking about. (**Devant vous, il y a le séjour. A droite, c'est la cuisine. A votre gauche, c'est le couloir qui mène aux trois petites chambres.**)

2. **Reading:** As a pre-reading activity, have students list the rooms and features they would like to have in a home or apartment. Distribute the floor plans. Have students skim each floor plan to determine which one meets their requirements. Have them add any new items they find to their lists. Explain any abbreviations the students don't understand: **PL (placard)** *closet,* **WC** *lavatory,* **S. d'E. (Salle d'eau)** *shower room,* **S. de B. (Salle de bains)** *bathroom,* **edf (Electricité de France)** *electrical hookup,* **Rang (Rangement)** *storage closet.*

3. **Speaking:** Have partners take turns giving prospective buyers or tenants a tour of the apartment or house represented by one of the floor plans. The realtor should point out the location of each room and some of the special features included. The buyer or tenant should ask questions and make comments.

4. **Speaking:** Have students work in pairs to play the game "20 Questions." One student chooses a floor plan. The other student tries to find out which floor plan the first student has chosen by asking only yes-no questions. (**Il y a au moins trois chambres? La cuisine est près de l'entrée?**) You might limit one round to five questions. Then have partners change roles and play another round.

Using Realia: Chapter 2

5. **Speaking:** Have students work in pairs with the floor plans. They should decide what furniture items they would like to place in each room and tell where they will place each item.

6. **Writing:** Have students create their own floor plans and label them.

7. **Culture:** Bring in floor plans of apartments or houses in your area. Have students compare the floor plans you bring in to the French floor plans. Ask them to point out any differences they might notice. Remind students of the **Note culturelle** on page 42 of the *Pupil's Edition* which mentions that many people in France use armoires instead of closets to store clothing.

Using Realia 2-3: Real estate ads

1. **Listening:** Make an announcement in the form of a recorded message describing one of the homes. Have students decide which ad it is.

2. **Reading:** Distribute the real estate ads. Have students read the ads and make a list of the abbreviations used. Have them write down what they think the abbreviations stand for and discuss each one.

3. **Reading:** Have students list information they would expect to find in a real estate advertisement. Have students read the ads and create a chart that compares the ads: number of rooms, size of certain rooms, number of bathrooms, special features **(piscine, belle architecture)**, price, and so on.

4. **Speaking:** Ask students to prepare a radio advertisement or a realtor's sales pitch to a prospective buyer or renter for one or two of the properties.

5. **Writing:** Have students write a real estate advertisement for a famous house/place such as the home of a TV/movie family or another famous building. Have their classmates try to guess what house/place they're describing.

6. **Writing:** Have students write a description of their own home or an imaginary home. They should include a description of the floor plan, tell what their favorite room is, and describe how it is furnished.

7. **Culture:** Have students locate on a map of France, the cities where the different houses advertised are located. Then have students research the name of the region where these cities are found (Brittany) and some details about its history and culture.

REALIA

A l'épicerie

Biscuits

Crackers salés, 75 g..................	**0,53**
Crackers fromage, 75 g	**0,53**
Feuilletés au fromage, 110 g	**0,71**
Snacks arachide, 50 g	**0,35**
Assortiment biscuits salés, 250 g...	**1,05**

Charcuterie

Jambon, le kg.....................	**8,05**
Saucisses de Strasbourg, le kg	**3,55**
Saucisses cocktail, le kg	**4,12**
Saucisson à l'ail, le kg.............	**3,35**
Rillettes de Tours, 200 g	**1,03**
Pâté de campagne, 340 g..........	**1,36**
Pâté de foie, 340 g................	**1,40**

Lait, crémerie

Lait écrémé, 1 litre	**0,53**
Lait 1/2 écrémé, 1 litre	**0,56**
Lait entier, 1 litre	**0,63**
Beurre pasteurisé des 2 Sèvres, 250 g	**0,95**
Beurre pasteurisé, 250 g..........	**0,85**
Beurre 1/2 sel breton, 500 g	**1,85**
Œufs extra frais, les 6	**0,69**

Eaux minérales, boissons

Cidre breton, 97 cl................	**0,59**
Jus de pomme, 1 litre.............	**0,49**
Jus d'orange, 1 litre..............	**0,95**
Coca, 1 litre.....................	**0,79**
Coca, pack de 6	**1,35**

Conserves de poissons

Sardines à l'huile d'arachide, 1/6 ...	**0,53**
Sardines à l'huile d'olive, 1/6	**0,54**
Sardines à la tomate, 1/6	**0,37**
Anchois en filets, 1/15.................	**0,48**
Maquereaux au vin blanc, 1/4........	**0,56**
Thon entier à l'huile, 1/10............	**0,69**
Thon entier à l'huile d'olive, 1/10 ...	**0,79**

Sucre

Sucre morceau n° 4, kg	**0,67**
Sucre semoule, kg	**0,62**
Sucre cristallisé, kg.................	**0,60**
Sucre de canne roux, kg..............	**1,05**

Huile, vinaigre, condiment

Huile de maïs, 1 litre	**1,18**
Huile d'arachide, 1 litre	**1,52**
Huile végétale, 1 litre	**0,78**
Huile de tournesol, 1 litre	**1,00**
Huile d'olive vierge extra, 1 litre	**2,58**
Vinaigre de vin 6°, 1 litre.............	**0,37**

Conserves de légumes

Petits pois fins......................	
Petits pois très fins.................	**0,30**
Petits pois extra fins................	**0,52**
Petits pois extra fins et carottes 1/2	**0,60**
Maïs en grains US, 1/2	**0,42**
	0,47

Realia 3-2

Savoir vivre à table

Le début du repas. *On ne doit jamais commencer à manger avant la maîtresse de la maison.*

On ne coupe pas *son pain, on le rompt en petits morceaux et toujours avec les deux mains.*

On ne souffle pas *sur la soupe. On ne fait pas de bruit en la mangeant. On ne suce pas sa cuillère. On ne soulève pas l'assiette.*

On ne choisit pas. *On ne touche pas trois ou quatre morceaux avant de trouver le bon. On ne coupe pas dans un plat. On ne touche pas trop les fruits. Pour refuser d'un plat, un geste de la main suffit.*

On ne coupe pas *sa viande avec sa fourchette, ni non plus en tenant son couteau comme un stylo. On ne met pas le couteau et la fourchette de chaque côté de l'assiette, mais dans l'assiette, l'un à côté de l'autre, et jamais en croix. On ne coupe pas œufs, gnocchis, nouilles, légumes, salades, gâteaux et glaces au couteau.*

Légumes et poissons. *Faire toujours attention aux légumes qui peuvent rebondir, aux sauces qui risquent d'éclabousser, aux coquillages ou aux poissons capables de rejaillir.*

Les fruits. *On coupe tout fruit en quatre, on le pèle au bout de la fourchette dans l'assiette.*

On ne boit pas *en renversant la tête et à grandes gorgées. On s'essuie la bouche avant et après avoir posé les lèvres contre le verre.*

Adapted from "Savoir vivre à table" from *Le Savoir-Vivre* by Gisèle d'Assailly and Jean Baudry. Copyright © by **Marabout.** Reprinted by permission of the publisher.

27 mai FETE DES MERES

boutique

Parapluie, 100 % coton – manche en bois – dessins et couleurs assortis **12 €**

Foulard 100 % polyester – 80 x 80 cm – dessins et couleurs assortis **6 €**

Foulard 100 % coton – 75 x 75 cm – dessins et couleurs assortis **4,50 €**

Foulard "pure soie" – 80 x 80 cm – dessins et couleurs assortis **11,50 €**

Echarpe voile, 100 % polyester – 40 x 160 cm – dessins et couleurs assortis **7,75 €**

Sac ou pochette – cuir véritable – séparation intérieure – bandoulière amovible – modèles assortis **22 €**

Sac tissu vinylique enduit – séparation intérieure – bandoulière amovible – couleurs assorties **20 €**

Grand sac croûte velours – fermeture par glissière – bandoulière amovible – poignées incorporées – couleurs assorties **17 €**

la maison

Service à fondue bourguignonne
comprenant : 1 pot à queue avec couvercle, fonte émaillée – couleur : uni 6 fourchettes – 1 réchaud avec plateau **32 €**

Using Realia: Chapter 3

Using Realia 3-1: Grocery price list

1. **Listening:** Focusing on one section of the ad at a time, make true-false statements concerning specific details about prices. **Les crackers salés coûtent 0,53 €. (Vrai) Les snacks arachide sont très chers. (Faux)**

2. **Reading:** As a pre-reading activity, have students list as many kinds of food stores as they can recall (**le supermarché, la boulangerie,** and so on). Then have students list items they might purchase in a grocery store (**l'épicerie**). Next, distribute copies of the ad and have students determine which items on their list are available at this store. Then have students name food items that aren't available at this store and tell where they would go to buy them.

3. **Speaking:** Have students use the information in the ads to act out various situations, such as purchasing items in the store or offering, accepting, refusing, and complimenting food served at a meal.

4. **Speaking:** Have partners interview each other concerning the items they prefer in each section of the **épicerie. (Tu aimes mieux le jambon ou les saucisses?)**

5. **Writing:** Have groups of students prepare true-false statements which they will use to test the comprehension of another group.

6. **Writing:** Have students prepare an ad for their favorite section(s) of a supermarket. Encourage them to include drawings of the products or pictures clipped from newspaper advertisements. Make sure they include descriptions, quantities, and prices of the individual products.

7. **Culture:** In France and other francophone countries, people generally purchase their groceries at small specialized shops and markets found in their neighborhood. They can walk to the local food stores and purchase their groceries on a daily basis. Ask students to think of the differences in how they would do their grocery shopping in France as opposed to how they might shop in the U.S. (For example, they might need to take along a **panier** or **caddie®** to carry their groceries since they will be going from store to store on foot). Have students name which items available at the **épicerie** they could also buy at specialty stores. Then ask them which items they might want to buy that aren't available at the **épicerie** and where they would go to get those items.

8. **Culture/Writing:** Write out a shopping list composed of various grocery items that would require trips to the **épicerie** as well as specialty stores. Have students write the order in which they would do their shopping, telling which store they will shop at first and what items they will buy at that store, which store they will shop at next, and so on.

Using Realia 3-2: Table manners

1. **Listening:** Distribute the list of table manners and allow students time to scan the text. Then describe to the students several activities you might do at the dinner table. **(Je coupe ma viande avec ma fourchette. Je coupe mon fruit en quatre.)** Have students vote on whether each activity is good manners or bad manners according to the realia. Tabulate the votes for each activity on the board. Then have students check their answers by reading aloud the section of the list on table manners that pertains to your description.

French 2 Allez, viens!, Chapter 3

REALIA

2. **Reading:** Have students read the list of table manners and indicate whether they agree or disagree with each rule described.

3. **Speaking:** Have students work in groups to act out a scene in which one student arrives at the home of his or her host family in France. The other students should greet and welcome the visiting student appropriately and then advise him or her on French table manners before the whole family sits down for dinner.

4. **Speaking:** Have students work in groups to prepare and act out a scene from a French dinner party. One student should play the host or hostess and offer foods to the other students. The other students should ask for certain foods and accept or refuse any foods the host or hostess offers. Students can showcase good or bad table manners during their skits. If a group chooses to show bad table manners, you might have the rest of the class identify which activities were improper after the skit is over.

5. **Writing:** Have students write a list of American table manners for a group of French exchange students who will be attending an elegant welcome dinner the evening they arrive from France.

6. **Culture:** Have students compare the list of table manners in the realia to common table manners used in the U.S. Have students speculate about where they might find this kind of text in French and then give examples of places to find rules for table etiquette in the United States.

Using Realia 3-3: Mother's Day sale promotion

1. **Listening:** Make public address announcements in a store, advertising these items. (**ATTENTION mesdames et messieurs, pour notre promotion "Fête des Mères", nous vous proposons des foulards 100 % coton à 4,50 € seulement.**) Have students indicate which items you're referring to.

2. **Reading:** As a pre-reading activity, have students make a list of appropriate gifts for Mother's Day. Then distribute the advertisement and have students compare their lists with the items described here. Ask detailed comprehension questions. (**Combien coûte le foulard "pure soie"? Quel sac coûte 17 €? Comment est-il?**)

3. **Speaking:** Have students pair off and take turns asking and giving advice about one of the Mother's Day gifts from the ad. Have them make and reject several suggestions before reaching a decision.

4. **Speaking:** Have students act out a situation in which a son or daughter gives his or her mother one of the gifts from the ad. The son or daughter should extend best wishes and the mother should react appropriately to the gift.

5. **Writing:** Have students write an advertisement for a gift of their choice for Mother's Day or for another gift-giving occasion.

6. **Culture:** In France, Mother's Day is celebrated on the eighth Sunday after Easter, and Father's Day is two Sundays after Mother's Day. Have students figure out the dates on which Mother's Day and Father's Day fall this year in France.

Realia 4-1

LE CREOLE : UNE LANGUE QUI CHANTE

La langue officielle de la Martinique est bien entendu le français, mais tous les Martiniquais parlent aussi le créole, langue commune à bien des pays de la Caraïbe comme la Guadeloupe, la Guyane, la Dominique, Sainte-Lucie ou Haïti. Jadis dénigré et réservé aux gens des classes défavorisées, le créole retrouve peu à peu sa vraie place dans la culture locale. Langue orale avant tout, il est issu de la rencontre et de la fusion du vieux français avec le vieil anglais, des dialectes africains et du vieil espagnol; plus ce «quelque chose» dans la façon de le dire qui donne au créole une saveur incomparable. Imagé, coloré, harmonieux, le créole chante aux oreilles. Quelque méthodes et dictionnaires ont été publiés qui aident à se familiariser avec ses subtilités.

From "Le Créole: une langue qui chante" from *Martinique effeuillée* by **Dalila Daniel.** Published by Société de Distribution Caraïbes. Reprinted by permission of the author.

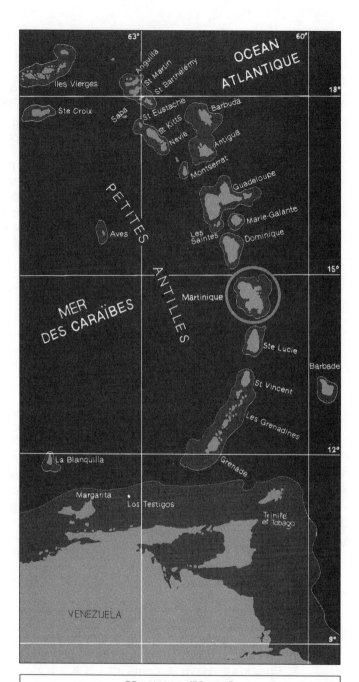

Martinique/*Matinik*		
Département Français *Départéman franssé*	Superficie/*Grandé:* 1080 km2	Montagne Pelée: *Roté la mont'n Pelée:* 1.397 m
Population/*Popilassion:* 350.000 habitants *350.000 moun'n*	Longueur/*Londjé:* 64 km	Piton Lacroix: *Roté Piton Lacroix:* 1.196 m
Fort-de-France: *Fod fransse:* 120.000 habitants *120.000 moun'n*	Largeur/*Lajé:* de 10 à 22 km *di 10 à 22 km*	

Map of the Petites Antilles from *Martinique* by Philippe and Didier Poux. Copyright © by **Editions Grand Sud.** Reprinted by permission of the publisher.

Les Zouk Machine

Après « Maldon », voici « Kréol », un nouvel album pour Dominique, Christiane et Jane, les trois « perles noires » venues de la Guadeloupe. Elles chantent « DJ », en hommage à tous les disc-jockeys qui lancent leurs chansons sur les pistes de danse.

Emmitouflées dans de grands manteaux, Jane, Dominique et Christiane, les trois « zoukettes » (leur surnom), du groupe Zouk Machine, s'habituent difficilement aux rigueurs de l'hiver métropolitain. « Aux Antilles, dit Jane, en plein hiver, on va à la plage et on se repose sous les palmiers. Le thermomètre, à moins de 14 degrés, c'est le froid polaire ! » Cet « éclat » évoque à Christiane des souvenirs d'enfance. « A l'époque, nous vivions en France, dans la banlieue nord de Paris. J'étais une toute petite fille et je pleurais sur le chemin de l'école tellement j'avais froid. Mon grand frère essayait de me consoler ! »

Ce « grand frère », Guy Houllier, est aujourd'hui, avec leur beau-frère, Yves Honoré, l'un des principaux auteurs-compositeurs du groupe. Jane, Dominique et Christiane leur doivent « Maldon », le succès de l'été 1990, longtemps numéro 1 du Top 50, et la plupart des chansons de leur nouvel album « Kréol », chez BMG. Elle chante notamment « D.J. », en hommage à tous les disc-jockeys qui lancent si bien leurs chansons.

« En réalité, Zouk Machine, c'est trois filles, deux leaders, Yves et Guy, et un groupe de musiciens. Nous travaillons en équipe en essayant d'harmoniser au mieux nos talents. Aux Antilles, Yves et Guy sont des musiciens respectés depuis des années. Ils ont un vrai sens de la composition. Notre point fort, c'est la voix. » Chacune a commencé sa carrière adolescente. Christiane a 13 ans quand elle devient choriste pour Expérience 7, le groupe de son frère. Encouragée à chanter par son père, amateur d'accordéon et d'harmonica, Dominique est remarquée par son professeur de chant lors d'une fête scolaire de fin d'année. Elle devient l'une des choristes les plus demandées des studios de Pointe-à-Pitre. Même parcours pour Jane qui, à l'occasion, défile aussi comme mannequin. Elles se rassemblent, en 1986, à la demande de Guy Houllier et Yves Honoré qui rêvent d'un trio féminin. Une première formule réunit Christiane, Dominique et Joëlle Ursull. Celle-ci s'en va au bout de six mois et Jane la remplace.

Sur le nouvel album, Guy et Yves leur ont confié la responsabilité d'écrire chacune une chanson. « Imaginer un texte n'est pas facile, une musique encore moins, avoue Dominique. J'ai ressorti la cassette de « Soulajé ké aw », un morceau que j'avais composé il y a plus d'un an. A l'époque, je pensais que jamais il ne les intéresserait. En l'écoutant, ils m'ont fait remarquer les points forts et les autres plus faibles. A partir de ma maquette, ils ont créé des arrangements. J'étais fière d'entendre le résultat.»

REALIA

From "Les Zouk Machine ont oublié Monsieur Bobo" by Cécile Tesseyre from *Télé 7 Jours*. Copyright © by Télé 7 Jours. Reprinted by permission of *Scoop*.

Realia 4-3

Tout pour faire votre toilette

Dentifrice
100 ml
1,30€

Savon
5 × 125g
2,40€

Brosse à dents
1,50€   souple,
médium,
dure ou
enfant

Serviettes
100% coton
100 × 150 cm   **12,65€**

Shampooing   **5€**
6 variétés au choix
le flacon de 500 ml

Réveil modèles assortis
garantie 1 an, pile
non-fournie
4,65€

Brosses à cheveux
et peignes de
1,45€ à 3,75€

Pyjama
100% soie, styles variés
22€

Using Realia 4-1: Le Créole

1. **Listening:** Have students scan the article about Creole. Then read a series of true-false statements telling which languages are spoken in certain countries. (**On parle créole en Martinique. On parle français en Italie,** and so on.) Have students call out **vrai** or **faux** according to each statement.

2. **Reading:** Distribute copies of the article and map. Allow students time to read the article. Then ask some comprehension questions. (Where is Creole spoken? Is Creole an oral or written language? What languages have influenced the development of Creole?)

3. **Speaking/Culture:** Have students work in groups. Have each group research one of the islands shown on the map of the Antilles. Then have each group present a description of the island in the form of a tourist advertisement to the rest of the class. Each group should describe the size of the island, its location, and its landscape.

4. **Writing/Culture:** Have students write a postcard to a French pen pal from one of the islands in the Caribbean. Students should first research the island to find out its major cities and tourist attractions. Students should include on their postcards a description of the island, based on their research.

5. **Culture:** Have students research why so many different languages are spoken in the Caribbean islands. You might divide the class into groups and assign a specific island or group of islands to each group. Have students present their findings to the rest of the class. You might want to prepare your own presentation about the history of the Caribbean islands in order to give your class a more complete view of the development of the area.

6. **Culture:** Have students research and compare the flora and fauna of continental France and Martinique. You might ask students what the department of Martinique has to offer France (exports, and so on) that its other departments on the continent might not have.

Using Realia 4-2: Les Zouk Machine

1. **Reading:** As a pre-reading activity, have students list the types of music and the groups they enjoy in English. Distribute the realia. Form small groups and assign a paragraph of the reading to each one. Have each group summarize the main idea and give one or two important supporting details.

2. **Listening:** Write the names of the members of **Zouk Machine** on the board. Make statements about the people or statements the people themselves might make. Have students identify the person the statement refers to or the speaker.

3. **Speaking:** Have students work in pairs. One student plays the role of a member of **Zouk Machine,** the other plays the role of a journalist. The students should act out an interview between the journalist and the musician. The interviewer should ask what the musician likes about his or her home in Martinique and what activities he or she likes to do there.

Using Realia: Chapter 4

4. **Writing:** Have students write a letter from one of the **Zouk Machine** musicians to a family member or friend back home in Martinique. They should describe what they like and dislike about Paris. They might also mention what they miss in Martinique. **(Ce qui me manque, c'est (de)...)**

5. **Culture:** Have students research music in Martinique. They might look for other bands which are popular for **zouk** music, or other types of music that are popular in Martinique. You might have students research the kinds of musical instruments used in music from Martinique. Students could compare their findings to the instruments used in a typical North American musical group.

Using Realia 4-3: Advertisement for toilet articles

1. **Listening:** Remove the prices from the copying master of the advertisement and distribute copies. Then tell students to write the price of each item as you read them aloud in a random order. Show a transparency of the advertisement with the prices included so students can check their answers.

2. **Listening:** Distribute copies of the advertisement. Read aloud some statements about your daily routine or activities. **(Je me lève à 7 heures.)** Students should write the statement next to the item in the advertisement that corresponds to the activity.

3. **Reading:** Distribute copies of the advertisement. Have students underline the cognates used in the descriptions of the items and provide translations. Have partners compare papers to learn from each other.

4. **Reading:** Have students read the descriptions of the items in the advertisement and circle any words they don't know. Then have volunteers write the unknown words on the board. Have the class brainstorm possible meanings for each word using the advertisement and its context.

5. **Speaking:** Before doing this activity do some pronunciation practice using the names of the items in the advertisement. Then have students work in pairs. One student should name one of the items. His or her partner should respond by naming the activity with which the item is associated.

6. **Speaking:** Have students work in pairs. One student should describe his or her morning routine and use the names of some of the items in the advertisement. The other student should check off every item his or her partner uses in a correct sentence. Then have students change roles.

7. **Writing:** Have students make a list of activities describing their daily routine. Then under each activity heading, have students write the names of the items from the advertisement that correspond to each category.

8. **Culture:** Have students convert the prices of the items in the advertisement into dollars and compare these prices with the prices of similar articles in the United States.

9. **Culture:** Have students read the descriptions of the shampoo and the soap. Ask them to brainstorm possible meanings for **ml** and **g.** Then remind them that in France liquids are measured in liters and milliliters, and weights are measured in grams and milligrams. Have them figure out the equivalent in fluid ounces.

French 2 Allez, viens!, Chapter 4

COLLÈGE, MODE D'EMPLOI

Tous les trucs pour devenir un collégien averti, et passer le meilleur des séjours sur la planète collège.

PENSEZ AU CAHIER DE TEXTES!

Deux trucs pour vous simplifier la vie :
Truc N° 1 : écrivez toujours très clairement les devoirs à faire–ce serait bête que vous ne compreniez plus le sujet de votre rédaction...
Truc N° 2 : n'attendez pas d'être lundi soir pour ouvrir la page de mardi. N'hésitez pas à prendre de l'avance chaque fois que possible.

GOÛTEZ D'ABORD, TRAVAILLEZ ENSUITE

Prenez le temps de souffler après l'école. Goûtez, jouez, détendez-vous un moment avant de vous mettre à vos devoirs. Vous travaillerez plus facilement et... plus efficacement.

PRÉVOYEZ LE P'TIT CREUX DE 11H

Il est important de prendre un vrai bon petit déjeuner parce que les matinées sont parfois longues au collège.
Et au cas où, glissez une pomme dans votre cartable.

CONFIEZ-VOUS, ÇA IRA MIEUX

Parfois les choses ne vont pas forcément comme on voudrait : on a du mal à suivre en techno, on se sent un peu seul(e), on a peur de ne pas y arriver... Tout le monde a ressenti ça, un jour ou l'autre.
Ce n'est pas très grave. Tournez-vous vers quelqu'un en qui vous avez confiance : votre grand-père, votre mère, un camarade, votre professeur principal, votre délégué de classe... Vous verrez, ça va tout de suite mieux lorsqu'on en parle...

CARBUREZ EN DORMANT

Le saviez-vous ? On retient toujours mieux ses leçons lorsqu'on les relit une fois ou deux, juste avant de s'endormir. Mais il faut bien sûr les avoir déjà un peu apprises avant...

GARDEZ LE MEILLEUR POUR LA FIN

Pourquoi ne pas commencer vos devoirs par la matière que vous aimez le moins... ou par l'exercice que vous trouvez le plus difficile ? D'accord, ce n'est pas très rigolo. Mais il faudra bien le faire, ce travail. Alors autant y aller directement, non ?
L'avantage ? On est toujours plus concentré au début des devoirs qu'à la fin. On a les idées plus claires, on comprend mieux. Et on finit par s'améliorer...
C'est pourquoi cette matière que vous n'appréciez pas deviendra peut-être celle que vous aimerez le plus...
Maintenant, si vous n'y arrivez vraiment pas, passez à autre chose. Vous y reviendrez plus tard.

REALIA

Adapted from "Collège, mode d'emploi" from "Le guide du collège," an insert from *Okapi*, no. 612. Copyright © by **Bayard Presse International**. Reprinted by permission of the publisher.

Realia 5-2

BILLET DE RETARD

NOM.. LE ....

PRENOM... ELEVE DE.................

ARRIVE(E) A .... AVEC.......... MINUTES DE RETARD

POUR LE MOTIF SUIVANT...

PEUT ETRE ADMIS(E) EN CLASSE...

DOIT ALLER EN ETUDE...

Signature du censeur :

DISPENSE D'EDUCATION PHYSIQUE

Je demande que mon enfant..

classe .... soit dispensé(e) **exceptionnellement**

du cours d'éducation physique et sportive

le.......................... de .... heures à............. heures.

Motif : ....

....

....

....

Signature(s) des parents :

*Visa
du professeur :*

*Visa
de l'établissement :*

BULLETIN D'ABSENCE

NOM.. LE ....

PRENOM... ELEVE DE.................

A ETE ABSENT(E) DEPUIS LE....................... A............... HEURES

POUR LE MOTIF SUIVANT ....

....

IL/ELLE RENTRERA LE........................... A............... HEURES

Signature(s) des parents :

MINISTERE DE L'EDUCATION NATIONALE   ACADEMIE DE TOURS

Collège **LA BUCAILLE — TOURS**

BULLETIN TRIMESTRIEL

Année scolaire : .... - .... trimestre

NOM et Prénom : ....   **Classe de** ....

MATIERES	NOTES	OBSERVATIONS
Français		
Mathématiques		
....		
....		
Sc. Physiques....................		
Sc. Naturelles		
Histoire -		
Géographie		
Langue Vivante 1		
L. V. 2		
....		
....		
Arts Plastiques..................		
....		
Education Musicale		
Travaux Manuels................		
Education Physique.............		
....		

Appréciation générale du Chef d'Etablissement :

Using Realia: Chapter 5

Using Realia 5-1: Article about preparing for school

1. **Listening:** Distribute copies of the article to the class. Allow students several minutes to scan the article to get the main idea of each section. Then read aloud a statement to summarize each of the six sections. **(Prenez un bon petit déjeuner. Commencez vos devoirs par un sujet que vous n'aimez pas.)** Have students number the paragraphs according to the order of your statements.

2. **Reading:** Distribute copies of the article. Have students work in pairs to figure out the main idea of each section of the article. Have students volunteer to share their findings with the whole class.

3. **Reading:** Have students read the article to determine the main idea of each section and how important they think the information is. Then have students work in groups or pairs to rate each section in order of importance, 1 being the most important idea and 6 being the least important idea. Have each group share their ratings with the rest of the class.

4. **Speaking:** Have students work in pairs. One student tells about an awful school day he or she had. The other student offers advice based on the information in the article.

5. **Writing:** Have students write a journal entry in which they describe a bad day they've had at school and then list some resolutions based on the advice in the article.

6. **Writing:** Have students work in groups. Together they should summarize the article and make a list of the major points. You might have each group prepare their summary as a news story that could be published in the school newspaper.

7. **Writing:** Have each student make two lists based on the information in the article. One list should show the activities suggested by the article that the student already practices. The second list should show the activities that the student does not regularly practice. You might follow up by having students share the information on their lists and offer each other congratulations or encouragement.

8. **Culture:** Ask students if they know what grade levels **Collège** refers to (junior high). Then ask students if they think the information in the article is useful for high school students. You might have students brainstorm advice they would add to the article that would be important for high school students.

Using Realia 5-2: School forms

1. **Reading:** Distribute copies of the school forms. Have students read each document and determine in what situation each would be used. Also have them determine who would most likely fill out the form and who needs to sign it.

2. **Listening:** Make numbered statements giving excuses, reasons for being late, and so on. **(1. J'ai raté le bus. 2. J'ai été malade pendant trois jours.)** Have students write the numbers on the appropriate forms. You may want to introduce some supplementary vocabulary found on pages 189-191 of the *Pupil's Edition* to further expand this activity.

3. **Writing:** Have students complete the forms, using information about themselves or about an imaginary student.

4. **Speaking:** Have students work in pairs to create a conversation based on one of the documents. Some conversations might involve: 1) a student explaining to a supervisor why he or she is late and needs a pass, 2) a child trying to convince his or her parent that he or she should be excused from gym, or 3) a student explaining to a teacher why he or she will be absent from school. Have students change roles and situations.

5. **Culture:** Bring to class several copies of your school's version of these three forms. Ask students how they are similar or different. Have students work in groups of three to create one new form that might be used in place of the three forms.

Using Realia 5-3: Report card

1. **Listening:** Read aloud grades and comments for an imaginary student. Have students fill in the report card based on the information they hear.

2. **Reading:** As a pre-reading activity, have students list in French as many school subjects as they can recall. Distribute the report card. Have students read the subjects on the report card and check off those that are either on their list or that are closely related to the ones on their list.

3. **Speaking:** Have students work in pairs to create a conversation between a parent or a teacher and the student whose report card they completed in the listening activity above. Partners can discuss the grades, offer praise or criticism, explain why the grade was received, offer advice for the next trimester, and so on.

4. **Writing:** Distribute a blank copy of the report card. Have students fill in the header information of ***Bulletin Trimestriel*** and the grades they think they would receive for each course. Then have students exchange papers with a partner and fill in the appropriate comments for each course.

5. **Culture:** Tell students that **L. V. 2** stands for **Langue Vivante 2.** Then have students brainstorm reasons why the French education system would require two foreign languages in the curriculum. Then have them brainstorm reasons why knowledge of several languages would be an asset in Europe. Finally, have them brainstorm reasons why it would be an advantage to learn several languages here in the United States.

REALIA

Realia 6-1

A l'extérieur du Château de Chenonceau

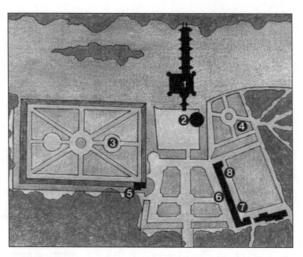

❶ Château
❷ Tour des Marques
❸ Jardin de Diane
❹ Jardin de Catherine

❺ Chancellerie
❻ Bâtiment des Dômes
❼ Musée de Cires
❽ Restaurant/Salon de thé

PRESENTATION DES JARDINS

Du balcon du premier étage, la vue s'étend sur la plus belle partie du domaine. A gauche, le Jardin de Catherine, aménagé en bordure du parc. Au centre, et immédiatement devant le château, la Cour d'Honneur que précède l'avant-cour à laquelle on accède par la Grande Allée bordée de platanes. Dans la Cour d'Honneur, la Tour des Marques commémore le souvenir de la famille des Marques, propriétaire de la Seigneurie de Chenonceau, au XVe siècle. A gauche, et bordant l'avant-cour, le bâtiment des Dômes qui correspond aux anciens communs. A droite, à l'entrée du Jardin de Diane, la Chancellerie, construite à la fin du XVIe siècle.

GALERIE

La Galerie, longue de soixante mètres, traverse le Cher.

Elle fut édifiée par Catherine de Médicis, très probablement d'après les plans de Philibert de l'Orme qui avait déjà bâti le pont construit par Diane de Poitiers.

Au cours de l'occupation allemande, de 1940 à 1942, de nombreuses personnes mirent à profit la situation privilégiée de la Galerie dont la porte sud donnait accès à la zone libre alors que l'entrée du Château se trouvait en zone occupée...

From the brochure *Château de Chenonceau*. Reprinted by permission of *Château de Chenonceau*.

A l'intérieur du Château de Chenonceau

CHAPELLE

En entrant dans la chapelle, veuillez remarquer la porte originale du XVIᵉ siècle. Les vitraux sont modernes : les anciens ont été détruits par un bombardement en 1944. Dans la loggia à droite : un marbre de CARRARE du XVIᵉ siècle. Sur les murs, sous les plaques de verre, des inscriptions laissées par des Gardes Ecossais : les plus anciennes datent de 1543. Au-dessus de la porte : la tribune d'où les Reines assistaient à la messe.

SALLE DE DIANE DE POITIERS

Cette pièce fut la chambre de Diane de Poitiers à qui Henri II avait fait don de Chenonceau. L'illustre favorite du Roi fit de nombreux séjours en son château qu'elle ne cessa d'embellir.

En 1559, à la mort de Henri II, tué en combat singulier lors d'un tournoi par le capitaine de ses Gardes Ecossais, Gabriel MONTGO-MERY, Catherine de Médicis se fit restituer le Château par Diane et lui donna en échange le Château de Chaumont-sur-Loire.

CABINET VERT

Cabinet de travail de Catherine de Médicis, cette pièce évoque le souvenir de la Reine Mère qui fit à Chenonceau de multiples séjours alors qu'elle était Régente du Royaume.

Le plafond est original : il n'a jamais été retouché depuis le XVIᵉ siècle. Au-dessus de la cheminée : SAMSON déchirant le lion, par GOLSIEUS. Sur le côté, une tapisserie du XVIᵉ siècle d'une couleur extrêmement rare : verte à l'origine, elle a pris en vieillissant une teinte bleue. Au-dessus de la porte, le grand tableau représentant "la Reine de Saba visitant Salomon" est de l'Ecole de Véronèse.

LIBRAIRIE

La petite pièce qui fait suite était la librairie de Catherine de Médicis : le plafond date de 1521 : c'est le plus ancien plafond du château. Au-dessus de la porte, "la Sainte-Famille" d'Andréa del Sarto. Sur le côté, "une martyre" par LE CORREGE.

CHAMBRE DE CATHERINE DE MEDICIS

Les tapisseries qui ornent les murs sont de la fin du XVIᵉ siècle. De la fenêtre percée au midi, on découvre la façade est du château. La famille MENIER, propriétaire de Chenonceau depuis 1913, vient d'y faire effectuer d'importantes restaurations destinées à sauvegarder l'aspect original de la façade dont les balcons et les lucarnes ont dû être entièrement remaniés.

SALON

Sur la cheminée : "la Salamandre" et "l'Hermine" évoquent le souvenir de François 1ᵉʳ et de Claude de France. A gauche de la cheminée : "Louis XIV", par Rigaud : ce tableau fut offert par le Roi lui-même, en souvenir d'une visite faite au Château : le cadre très curieux est fait de quatre pièces de bois.

CUISINES

Aménagées dans les deux piles du château ancrées dans le lit du Cher, les cuisines témoignent de l'art et de l'ingéniosité des bâtisseurs de la Renaissance.

Vous y accéderez en empruntant l'escalier qui les dessert, au fond du vestibule, juste avant l'entrée de la galerie.

From the brochure *Château de Chenonceau*. Reprinted by permission of **Château de Chenonceau**.

REALIA

excursions
services de
tourisme SNCF

CHATEAUX DE LA LOIRE

Circuits en autocars au départ de TOURS

Départ à 9 h 00, place de la Gare, quai n° 6

1 - TOURS, Cormery, vallée de l'Indre, **LOCHES** (visite, déjeuner libre), **CHENONCEAU** (visite), **AMBOISE** (visite), Montlouis, TOURS (vers 18 h 45).

Les samedis, du 10 avril au 25 septembre. **Car : 22 €**
Les mardis, du 6 juillet au 28 septembre. **Droits d'entrée : 10 €**

2 - TOURS, Luynes, Cinq-Mars-la-Pile, **LANGEAIS** (visite), **USSÉ** (visite), Chinon (déjeuner libre), **AZAY-LE-RIDEAU** (visite), **VILLANDRY** (visite des jardins), TOURS (vers 18 h 45).

Les mercredis et dimanches, **Car : 22 €**
du 11 avril au 29 septembre. **Droits d'entrée : 12 €**

3 - TOURS, Amboise (vue sur le château), Chaumont, **BLOIS** (visite, déjeuner libre), Ménars, **CHAMBORD** (visite), **CHEVERNY** (visite), vallée du Cher, TOURS (vers 18 h 45).

Les lundis et vendredis, **Car : 22 €**
du 12 avril au 27 septembre. **Droits d'entrée : 10 €**

4 - TOURS, **CHENONCEAU** (visite), **AMBOISE** (visite, déjeuner libre), **CHAUMONT** (visite), vallée de la Loire, **VOUVRAY** (visite), TOURS (vers 18 h 30).

Les jeudis, du 15 avril au 30 septembre. **Car : 22 €**
Droits d'entrée : 9,50 €

Départ à 13 h 15, place de la Gare, quai n° 6

5 - TOURS, vallée de l'Indre, **SACHÉ,** demeure de Balzac (visite), **AZAY-LE-RIDEAU** (visite), **VILLANDRY** (visite des jardins), TOURS (vers 18 h 30).

Les jeudis du 1er juillet au 9 septembre. **Car : 15 €**
Droits d'entrée : 9 €

6 - TOURS, **CHENONCEAU** (visite), **AMBOISE** (visite), **VOUVRAY** (visite), TOURS (vers 19 heures).

Le 11 avril.
Les mardis, du 13 avril au 29 juin.
Les dimanches, du 30 mai au 26 septembre.
Les mercredis, du 7 juillet au 8 septembre. **Car : 15 €**
Les vendredis, du 2 juillet au 27 août. **Droits d'entrée : 7 €**

7 - TOURS, Vouvray, **CHAUMONT** (visite), **LE CLOS-LUCÉ** à Amboise, demeure de Léonard de Vinci (visite), **MONTLOUIS** (visite), TOURS (vers 18 h 45).

Les samedis, du 3 juillet au 11 septembre. **Car : 15 €**
Droits d'entrée : 6 €

8 - TOURS, Savonnières, Villandry, **USSÉ** (visite), **LANGEAIS** (visite), TOURS (vers 18 heures).

Les mardis, du 6 juillet au 11 septembre. **Car : 15 €**
Droits d'entrée : 5 €

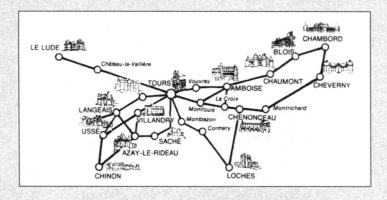

RENSEIGNEMENTS, RESERVATIONS, BILLETS

- **Services Touristiques de Touraine**
  Bureau Circuits Châteaux de la Loire
  Gare S.N.C.F. de Tours Tél. 02 47 05 46 09
  Place Maréchal-Leclerc
  de 8 h à 11 h et de 15 h 30 à 19 h
  Fermé l'après-midi des dimanches et jours fériés.

- Accueil de France Tél. 02 47 05 58 08
  (Office de Tourisme) Télex 750 008

- Bureau de Tourisme de la S.N.C.F.
  et principales Agences de Voyages

Libérez-vous de tous les soucis et bénéficiez du tarif "groupes" pour les entrées dans les châteaux, en participant à nos circuits organisés.

Adapted from "Circuits d'une journée," adapted from "Circuits d'une demi-journée," "Renseignements, Réservations, Billets," and tour map from *Châteaux de la Loire.* Reprinted by permission of *Services Touristiques de Touraine.*

REALIA

Nom_____ Classe_____ Date_____

Using Realia 6-1: Outside the Chenonceau château

1. **Listening:** Choose a place on the map and imagine you're standing in that place. Tell what you can see on your right, on your left, next to you, in front of you, and what you're doing there. **(Que c'est beau ici! Il y a des fleurs magnifiques. A gauche, il y a la Tour des Marques. Derrière moi, c'est le salon de thé.)** Have students write down the number of the place where you're standing.

2. **Reading:** Distribute the castle guide. Have students read the text with a partner. Have them imagine they're on the balcony of the château (number 1), looking out at the grounds of the château. One partner covers up the map legend while the other partner asks him or her what is located at each number on the map.

3. **Reading:** Have students scan the descriptions of the Chenonceau castle and underline all the dates they find. Then have them read closely the sentences in which the dates are given to determine why each date is mentioned. Finally, have students sketch a time line marking the dates and important events.

4. **Speaking:** Have students work in pairs. One student should give a guided tour of the grounds of Chenonceau. The other student should react to the tour by expressing enthusiasm, indifference, or dissatisfaction.

5. **Writing:** As a pre-writing activity, have students make a list of the activities they could do while visiting the castle. Then have students write a postcard to a friend or family member describing the Chenonceau castle, what they did on their visit to the castle, and what it was like.

6. **Culture:** Bring in a map that shows how France was divided during the German occupation in WWII. Have students locate the Chenonceau castle on this map in order to illustrate the situation described in the realia. Have students locate on the map other castles of the Loire region (Amboise, Azay-le-Rideau, Chinon, Loches, Ussé, Villandry, and so on) to determine whether they were occupied by the German army or remained free during World War II.

Using Realia 6-2: Inside the Chenonceau château

1. **Reading:** As a pre-reading activity, have students suggest the kinds of things they would expect to see in a guided tour of a château. Distribute the castle guide. Assign each room to a group of students. Have them read the description to determine the history of the room, what it was used for, important furnishings in the room, and so on. Have each group read the description again and select one or two important features to share with the class.

2. **Listening:** Read statements that a tour guide would make. Have students try to guess what room the guide is describing.

3. **Speaking:** Have students pair off and choose one of the descriptions. Tell them to imagine they're touring the château together. One of them has a guide book (the realia page). As one asks questions about a particular room of the château, the other refers to the castle guide to answer. Partners should change roles several times during the activity.

REALIA

Using Realia: Chapter 6

4. **Speaking:** Have students work in pairs. One student should tell the other about a trip he or she took to the Chenonceau castle, using the past tense. The other student should react appropriately. Then students should change roles. Each student should describe the activities that he or she did and which parts of the castle he or she liked the most.

5. **Writing:** Have students write a letter to a pen pal describing their trip to the Chenonceau castle. The letter should tell what activities they did while visiting the castle and what parts of the castle most impressed them.

6. **Culture:** Have students scan the text and name the persons who are associated with the Chenonceau castle. You might have students research who built and lived in some of the other castles in the Loire region. Then have students work together to create a family tree of the French royal family.

Using Realia 6-3: Tour bus schedule

1. **Listening:** Distribute copies of the bus schedule and allow students time to scan the document. Then pick a tour and read aloud the sequence of stops the bus makes. **(Je pars de Tours. D'abord, je vais à Cormery, puis à la vallée de l'Indre,** and so on.) Have students call out the number of the tour you're describing as soon as they recognize it. Remind students that some of the tours may only differ by one or two stops.

2. **Listening:** Make a series of true-false statements. **(Le tour numéro 2 va à Ménars.)** Have students raise their right hands when they hear a true statement and their left hands when they hear a false statement.

3. **Reading:** Have students scan the bus schedule. Point out that there are two prices listed under each tour description. Have students tell the purpose for each price listing.

4. **Reading:** Have students read the bus schedule to determine which dates the tour buses are running. Have students name the months when there are no tour buses listed on the schedule. Ask students to imagine why this bus schedule is limited to specific months.

5. **Speaking:** Have students work in pairs. One student wants to buy a ticket and should ask for information about one of the tours on the schedule. The other student should tell about the tour based on the information on the schedule and sell his or her partner a ticket.

6. **Writing:** Have students write a letter to the **Services Touristiques de Touraine** in order to make reservations for one of the tours on the schedule. They should be sure to mention the number of the tour, the day they would like to take the tour, and specify the number of tickets they will need.

7. **Culture:** Have students work in groups or in pairs. Assign each group or pair a château to research. Have each group or pair present a brief in-class history of the château, telling who built it, who lived there, and so on, and what it is famous for today.

French 2 Allez, viens!, Chapter 6

REALIA

J'ai mal...
Et si c'était le stress?

TU N'ARRIVES PAS À DORMIR? TU TE TORDS DE DOULEUR RÉGULIÈREMENT SANS SAVOIR POURQUOI ? TU PERDS TES CHEVEUX OU ENCORE TU ES COUVERT DE BOUTONS ? TOUT CELA NE VIENT PEUT-ÊTRE QUE... DE TA TÊTE QUI RÉAGIT AU STRESS, À L'ANGOISSE OU BIEN À LA COLÈRE EN S'EN PRENANT À TON CORPS.

Relax, Max!

L'ennemi, c'est le stress. Et l'ennemi du stress, c'est la relaxation. Elle a pour effet de calmer la douleur, de favoriser le sommeil, de chasser les idées noires, d'aider à réfléchir. Voici quelques trucs pour te relaxer...

Respire. Allonge-toi et pose la main sur ton ventre. Tu vas inspirer par le nez et expirer par la bouche, lentement. A chaque fois, tu dois sentir ton ventre gonfler et dégonfler à fond. Cette respiration abdominale a des effets calmants formidables !

Décontracte tes muscles. Mets-toi debout, les jambes un peu écartées et fléchies. Cherche la position où tu vas te sentir bien. Tu vas te plier en deux, tout doucement, en commençant par baisser la tête, le cou, les épaules, les bras, etc. Reste dans cette position aussi longtemps que possible, en ne pensant qu'au bien-être qui envahit ton corps.

Ecoute de la musique. Il existe des CD conçus exprès pour favoriser la relaxation, avec de la musique douce et des sons de la nature. Mais une de tes musiques préférées, à condition qu'elle ne soit ni violente ni trop triste, fera l'affaire. Allonge-toi, tamise la lumière... et c'est parti!

Adapted from "J'ai mal... Et si c'était dans la tête?" (retitled "J'ai mal... Et si c'était le stress?") from *Bravo Girl*, no. 144. Copyright © by **Editions Bauer.** Reprinted by permission of the publisher.

REALIA

Realia 7-2

CLUB LAFLEUR
50 ACTIVITES QUI ONT DU SOUFFLE.

50 activités

Activité	AUTEUIL	CHAMPS-ELYSEES	DENFERT-ROCHEREAU	GRENELLE	LA DEFENSE	LAFAYETTE	MAILLOT	MONCEAU	MONTSOURIS	NATION	PLACE D'ITALIE	REPUBLIQUE	SAINT-QUENTIN	VAUGIRARD	VAUGIRARD JUNIOR	VELIZY
CARDIO-TRAINING vélo électronique, tapis de marche, tapis de jogging, rameur électronique	•	•	•	•	•	•	•	•	•	•	•	•	•		ACTIVITES SPECIALES JUNIOR DE 2 A 18 ANS	•
MUSCULATION musculation aux appareils, abdo-fessiers, rubber band	•	•	•	•	•	•	•	•	•	•	•	•	•			•
CULTURE PHYSIQUE culture physique, aérobic, low impact, aéro jazz, stretching, gym acrobatique, training forme, chromo-gym	•	•	•	•	•	•	•	•	•	•	•	•	•			•
RELAXATION yoga, gym douce	•	•	•	•												
DANSE danse classique, base classique, barres au sol, mime, modern jazz, claquettes, danse de salon, rock, rock acrobatique, danse orientale, danse africaine	•	•	•	•		•	•			•		•				
ARTS MARTIAUX aikibudo, aikido, judo, kendo, karaté, kung fu, tae kwon do, tai chi chuan, viet vo dao, kobudo bâton	•	•	•	•		•	•	•		•		•		•		
SPORTS AQUATIQUES natation, gym aquatique, gym évolutive	•		•	•					•	•	•					
PLEIN AIR jogging, cyclisme, planche à voile, roller skate	•		•	•		•		•								
SPORTS DE BALLE tennis, tennis de table, tenkit, badminton, golf	•	•	•	•	•	•					•	•	•	•		•

AUTEUIL   1 46 51 88 35
22, rue Chanez 16ᵉ
DENFERT-ROCHEREAU   1 45 42 50 12
82, avenue du Général Leclerc
Les Portiques d'Orléans 14ᵉ
GRENELLE   1 45 75 34 48
31, rue Fremicourt 15ᵉ
LA DEFENSE   1 47 78 70 09
Centre Commercial les 4 Temps Parvis
LAFAYETTE   1 48 74 58 33
1, rue de la Victoire 9ᵉ
MAILLOT   1 45 74 14 98
71, rue du Débarcadère 17ᵉ
MONCEAU   1 43 80 68 71
42, rue de Chazelles 17ᵉ
MONTSOURIS   1 45 89 36 20
37, rue Brillet Savaran 13ᵉ

NATION   1 42 45 03 76
61, rue des Colonnes du Trône 12ᵉ
PLACE D'ITALIE   1 45 80 34 39
Centre Galaxie
42, rue Vandrezanne 13ᵉ
REPUBLIQUE   1 47 00 28 44
10, rue de Malte 11ᵉ
ST-QUENTIN   1 30 57 40 15
Centre Commercial
Saint-Quentin-en-Yvelines
SALLE DES CHAMPS   1 45 62 99 09
65 bis, rue de Ponthieu 8ᵉ
VAUGIRARD JUNIOR   1 43 06 38 50
12, rue de l'Amiral Roussin 15ᵉ
VELIZY   1 39 56 87 36
14, avenue de l'Europe 78140 Vélizy
(face au Centre Commercial)

(Map showing locations: LA DÉFENSE, MONCEAU, LAFAYETTE, MAILLOT, SALLE DES CHAMPS, RÉPUBLIQUE, AUTEUIL, NATION, GRENELLE, VAUGIRARD, DENFERT-ROCHEREAU, PLACE D'ITALIE, VÉLIZY, ST-QUENTIN, MONTSOURIS)

REALIA

Nutrition
Guide alimentaire canadien pour une alimentation saine

Le guide alimentaire canadien classe les aliments en groupes selon leur valeur nutritive. Il a été conçu pour nous montrer quels sont les éléments nutritifs dont nous avons besoin quotidiennement et pour nous aider à bien choisir les aliments des 4 groupes alimentaires.

1. pain et céréales
2. fruits et légumes
3. produits laitiers
4. viande et substituts

Les produits céréaliers et les fruits et légumes devraient composer la majeure partie d'un régime alimentaire sain tandis que les produits laitiers et la viande ou ses substituts devraient y tenir une place moins importante.

Choisissez plus souvent:

- une variété d'aliments de chaque groupe tous les jours
- des aliments faibles en gras
- des produits de blé entier et des produits enrichis (augmentent les fibres)
- les légumes vert foncé et orange et les agrumes
- les produits laitiers faibles en matières grasses
- les viandes maigres, la volaille et le poisson, les pois secs, les haricots et les lentilles

Les aliments qui ne font pas partie des 4 groupes alimentaires forment la catégorie des Autres Aliments. Ce sont le beurre, la margarine, les huiles, les vinaigrettes, le sucre, les bonbons, les collations à haute teneur en gras et en sel, les sodas, les herbes, les épices et les condiments. Ces aliments peuvent venir s'ajouter au plaisir de manger sainement, ils contiennent cependant plus de graisses et sont plus caloriques. Ils doivent donc être consommés avec modération.

Ayez du plaisir à bien manger, débutez la journée avec un bon petit déjeuner, mangez à des heures régulières et prenez des collations saines entre les repas.

From "Nutrition: (3) Guide alimentaire canadien pour une alimentation saine." Online, World Wide Web. Available www.lung.ca/asthme/nutrition/guide.html. Reprinted by permission of *The Canadian Lung Association.*

R E A L I A

Using Realia: Chapter 7

Using Realia 7-1: Article about stress

1. **Listening:** Have students scan the article. Then read aloud some true-false statements about how to relieve stress. (**Pour chasser le stress, il faut respirer bien.**) Have students call out **vrai** or **faux** according to each sentence. You might call on volunteers to correct any false statements.

2. **Reading:** Have students read the advice offered for relieving stress. As they read through each suggestion have them act out each activity. You might want to bring in some relaxing music for the whole class to listen to when students get to the last suggestion.

3. **Speaking:** Have students work in pairs. One student should tell about a stressful day at school. The other should offer advice about how to relax based on the information in the article.

4. **Writing:** Ask students to imagine they have a friend who's feeling stressed about an upcoming exam. Have each student write a short letter describing what his or her friend can do to relieve stress. Students may add their own suggestions to the ones already in the article.

5. **Writing:** Have students work in groups to write a list of suggestions for other students who may be feeling stressed.

6. **Culture:** Ask students which French musicians they know of and whether or not their music would be appropriate to use for relaxation. Before doing this activity, you might have students research French music and create a list of musicians and their different styles of music.

Using Realia 7-2: Directory of fitness clubs

1. **Listening:** Distribute copies of the sports club directory, and tell students that this document shows the places around Paris where Club Lafleur has opened a gym. Explain to the students how the document is organized. Then name some activities you would like to do. (**Je veux faire de la natation.**) Ask students to mark the gyms where these activities are offered.

2. **Listening:** Distribute copies of the sports club directory and explain to students that each of the addresses includes a number referring to the **arrondissement** where it is located. Make true-false statements about the club addresses. (**Le Club Lafleur à la Place d'Italie est dans le 13e arrondissement.**) Have students raise their right hand when they hear a true statement and their left hand when they hear a false statement.

3. **Reading:** As a pre-reading activity, have students list the names of sports and activities that they think would be offered at a fitness club. Distribute the realia. Have students skim the activities offered at this club to find any they listed. Have them look for cognates and French words they already know. Ask comprehension questions. (**On peut faire de l'aérobic au club de Monceau? Quel club est le seul qui offre du golf?**)

4. **Speaking:** Have students work in pairs to create a conversation between friends who would like to start an exercise program. The students should discuss the activities they like, those they dislike, at which location(s) the activities are offered, how often they plan to go, and so on.

5. **Speaking:** Once the partners have decided on their activity program, have one of the students telephone the club that the partners have chosen to attend. The other student plays the role of an employee at the club. The student who telephones should ask questions about the activities, verify the address, and ask for the hours of operation and the club fees. The employee at the club should make up some typical hours of operation and prices.

6. **Writing:** Have students write an advertisement for one of the locations of **Club Lafleur**. The advertisement should promote the different kinds of activities available, give the address and telephone number, and offer a special 25% discount **(tarif réduit)** if people join by a certain date.

7. **Culture:** Distribute copies of the sports club directory and have students compare and contrast the activities offered at the gyms in France versus those offered at gyms in the U.S. Students may want to research other sports and activity centers on the Internet, such as a **Maison des jeunes et de la culture**.

Using Realia 7-3: Canadian food guide

1. **Listening:** Write on the board the names of the four food groups in French. Then read a list of various food items. For each food you name have students tell which food group it belongs to.

2. **Listening:** Distribute copies of the food guide and allow students time to scan the text. Then read aloud several sentences describing good and bad eating habits. Have students tell whether the activity you describe is **alimentation saine** or not.

3. **Reading:** Ask students to read the food guide. Then ask which foods are most important in a healthy diet and which foods should be consumed the least, according to the food guide.

4. **Speaking:** Have students work in pairs to act out a visit to a nutritionist. One student should describe his or her diet to the nutritionist. The nutritionist should advise against eating certain foods and recommend some ways the student might improve his or her diet.

5. **Writing:** Have students work in pairs or groups to write an article about teenagers' diets at their school. First, they should make a list of foods that teenagers at their school typically eat for lunch. Then students should advise against any typical foods that are unhealthy and encourage typical foods that are healthy.

6. **Writing:** Have students work in small groups to prepare a healthy menu for a dinner party. Students should use the food guide to help plan their appetizers, main courses, and desserts, and should include food items from every food group in their menu.

R E A L I A

LA RENTREE DES CLASSES
(extrait)

L'école était l'avant-dernière maison en allant vers la plage. La rentrée! Le matin, de bonne heure, les enfants débouchaient de tous les côtés, de tous les coins, de toutes les ruelles, avec des sacs sous le bras, des cerceaux en mains. L'école bruyante, mouvementée, animée revivait. Elle faisait penser au retour des tisserins[1] dans les palmiers. Sa volée de moineaux lui était revenue. Partout des chants, des appels, des cris. Les anciens se saluaient joyeusement, tandis que les nouveaux, dépaysés[2], cherchaient un maintien[3]. Tombés dans le monde des écoliers, désorientés, inquiets, ils s'accrochaient à leurs parents.

Ici, l'on jouait aux billes, là on s'ébattait, ailleurs, c'étaient des jeux de course, un peu plus loin, le saute-mouton, le colin-maillard, le football.

Voilà le directeur, un homme grand, à la démarche calme. A son approche, les bruits cessent. Il répond aux nombreux, « bonjour, Monsieur », sourit à tous, entre dans la salle de classe, passe le doigt sur le tableau noir, sur un banc, pose ses livres sur la table et se saisit d'une badine qu'il a fait couper. Il la plie... Elle est de race comme badine. Elle peut faire du bon travail, aider efficacement à inculquer[4] les rudiments[5] du français et des autres matières dans les esprits quelque peu bouchés.

Climbié serre son ardoise sous le bras et regarde le directeur qui vient de siffler. Les élèves accourent. Les anciens s'alignent devant leur classe tandis que les nouveaux se mettent à part. C'est l'appel. Et chaque élève entre à l'appel de son nom. Les nouveaux ne sont pas nombreux, l'exiguïté[6] des salles limite leur nombre. Des parents restent là, à supplier le directeur d'accepter leurs enfants qui, pleurant, refusent de s'en aller.

« – Il n'y a plus de place.

– Ils peuvent s'asseoir dans l'allée, rester debout, pourvu qu'ils apprennent quelque chose.

– Impossible, j'ai pris le maximum d'élèves.

– Alors que vont devenir les enfants refoulés de votre école?

– Comment voulez-vous que je le sache?

– Pourraient-ils avoir une place à Moussou, à Impérial?

– Je ne le pense pas. Mes collègues et moi sommes dans la même situation.

– Vous ne pouvez absolument rien pour eux?

– Hélas! »

Et le directeur impuissant regarde partir ces enfants. Il aurait voulu, d'un seul geste, agrandir cette école. Les deux bras aux chambranles[7] de la porte, il semble tenter l'épreuve. Mais les murs ne bougent pas. Le directeur regarde partir les parents et leurs enfants. A chaque rentrée, ce sont les mêmes scènes, le même spectacle.

Bernard B. Dadié, *Climbié*, Seghers.

---

[1] **tisserins** : oiseaux de l'ordre des passereaux, habiles à tisser leur nid. – [2] **dépayser** : faire changer de pays, désorienter. Ici, les nouveaux élèves sont un peu perdus. – [3] **maintien** : manière de se tenir, attitude. – [4] **inculquer** : apprendre à force de répéter. – [5] **rudiments** : premières notions. – [6] **exiguïté** : petitesse. – [7] **chambranles** : cadres d'une porte, d'une fenêtre.

Bernard Dadié: Auteur ivoirien, né en 1916, a étudié en Côte d'Ivoire et au Sénégal. Auteur de livres de poésie, de pièces de théâtre et de romans inspirés par des thèmes traditionnels de son pays, il a publié son premier roman, *Climbié,* en 1956. C'est un roman autobiographique qui représente l'Afrique du passé où la Côte d'Ivoire était toujours une colonie de la France. Le paragraphe ci-dessus commence un passage sur l'éducation des enfants africains dans le système scolaire français. Dadié habite actuellement en Côte d'Ivoire. En continuant d'écrire, il tient aussi une présence forte dans la politique de son pays.

A bâton rompu avec Aïcha,

Miss Côte d'Ivoire

Infos Magazine a décidé de vous faire revivre un événement attentivement suivi par tous les Ivoiriens : l'élection de MISS Côte d'Ivoire. Pour ce faire, nous avons rencontré en exclusivité celle qui représente la beauté et la féminité ivoirienne; **Mademoiselle Aïcha Kéita.**

Anne-Françoise EBAH
Rédacteur en Chef, Infos Magazine

Infos Magazine : Comment avez-vous eu l'idée de vous pré-senter au concours de MISS Côte d'Ivoire ?

"J'ai toujours été attirée et fascinée..."

Aïcha K. : J'ai toujours été attirée et fascinée par le milieu de la mode. Lorsque j'étais petite, j'adorais regarder, à la télévision, les défilés de mode, les concours de beauté, etc... Imiter les mannequins m'amusait beaucoup! En grandissant, j'ai eu des propositions pour faire des photos de mode et participer à des défilés; ça a toujours été un de mes passe-temps favoris. Et puis un jour, un de mes amis m'a suggéré de me présenter à l'élection de MISS Côte d'Ivoire. J'avoue que je n'ai pas dit oui tout de suite; j'ai quand même mis un an avant de me décider.

Infos Magazine : Pourquoi? Qu'est-ce qui vous a fait hésiter ?

Aïcha K. : Si j'ai mis autant de temps, c'est que je ne me sentais pas prête, ça ne me disait rien; et en plus, je savais que je devais préparer mon baccalauréat. Jamais j'aurais pu assumer mon rôle de MISS et préparer en même temps mes examens; tandis que cette année, mon élection a coïncidé avec la fin de mon année scolaire.

Infos Magazine : Vous venez de passer votre baccalauréat, qu'avez-vous l'intention de faire?

Aïcha K. : Des études de commerce.

Infos Magazine : Pensez-vous que vos projets soient compatibles avec vos responsabilités de MISS Côte d'Ivoire ?

Aïcha K. : J'ai eu mon examen tout en préparant le concours. Je ne pense pas que le rêve de MISS Côte d'Ivoire puisse gêner mes projets car je ne devrais intervenir qu'occasionnellement lors de certains galas ou de certaines manifestations, le reste du temps, je pourrais me consacrer à mes études; tout est une question d'organisation.

REALIA

Realia 8-3

UN MAGNIFIQUE PAYS DE CIRCUITS OÙ TOUS LES ITINÉRAIRES SONT POSSIBLES, MÊME LES PLUS SECRETS...

Un ensemble de circuits, diversifiés et complémentaires, font découvrir les multiples facettes de la mosaïque ivoirienne : du pays Baoulé, cœur de la Côte d'Ivoire, jusqu'aux forêts du Royaume Agni à l'est; du nord harmonieux des Sénoufos jusqu'aux hautes montagnes du pays Yacouba à l'ouest; des anciens comptoirs de la côte jusqu'aux anciennes capitales dont les vestiges et la mémoire appartiennent à l'histoire.

Alors, il faut "prendre son pied la route" : ce pays s'offre sans détour à ceux qui sauront le découvrir et l'aimer.

Côte d'Ivoire

LE PAYS YACOUBA

A l'ouest, dans la douceur du climat montagneux, c'est le pays étonnant des Yacoubas. Man, la ville aux 18 montagnes, repose dans un écrin de verdure et de cascades, avec ses fabuleux ponts de lianes dont la réalisation reste encore inexpliquée. La fascinante secte du Gor, ces grands initiés qui ont le pouvoir de se rendre invisibles ou de se métamorphoser en léopards, les acrobates masqués qui virevoltent sur d'immenses échasses, les fillettes parées s'élançant gracieusement sur des poignards tendus par des danseurs couverts de cauris...

Pagnes tissés, vannerie, sculpture sur bois, masques pour collectionneurs avertis sont les principales productions artisanales du pays Yacouba.

LE PAYS BAOULE

A la lisière de la forêt et de la savane, ce peuple de planteurs a fait de cette région centrale le poumon économique du pays. Au pied du mont Orumbo Boka, subsistent encore les puits d'où venait l'or qui a permis la prospérité des Baoulés et favorisé l'essor d'un artisanat très raffiné : batiks, poids Akan, masques en bois sculpté, bijoux en or...

YAMOUSSOUKRO : Village natal du Président Houphouët-Boigny. Depuis 1983 capitale administrative et politique. La ville est un pari : architecture d'avant-garde, marbre rose de l'Hôtel Président Sofitel qui domine l'un des plus beaux parcours de golf du monde, universités et grandes écoles aux lignes futuristes...

LA BASILIQUE DE LA BROUSSE : Superbe, généreuse, à couper le souffle! C'est une première mondiale par ses dimensions, les technologies utilisées, ses immenses vitraux à l'ancienne. Demain, Notre-Dame-de-la-Paix sera un haut lieu de la foi, de la paix et du tourisme ivoirien.

LE PAYS SENOUFO

Dans le climat sec du nord, la savane aux tons ocres est ponctuée de petits villages aux cases arrondies, avec de magnifiques portes en bois sculptées. C'est la région de l'harmonie, réglée par le Poro, l'initiation longue et complexe qui en 7 années fait un Homme d'un enfant. Hors de l'enceinte du bois sacré, c'est l'apparition de masques extraordinaires, inquiétants ou facétieux, toujours insolites, accompagnés du son mélodieux des balafons. Mondialement renommé, l'artisanat Sénoufo est riche de ses toiles peintes de Korhogo, de sa statuaire aux lignes épurées, de ses masques polychromes et de ses poteries.

LE ROYAUME AGNI

Le royaume Agni, ou Indénie, déploie ses fastes dans la grande forêt. Ici, l'histoire côtoie le merveilleux car ces petits royaumes ont mille légendes que racontent les griots : pourquoi les villageois de Soko cohabitent-ils avec les singes sacrés? Quelle est l'histoire de la rivière aux poissons sacrés de Sapia?... A Abengourou, le Roi des Agnis reçoit dans sa résidence traditionnelle, érigée en 1882. A Zaranou, un chef Agni accorde le privilège d'assister avec lui et ses notables aux danses réservées aux invités de passage. Les artisans Agnis réalisent des tapisseries stylisées (Abengourou), des statuettes et des objets en bronze à la cire perdue, des pagnes richement tissés.

From *Côte d'Ivoire: Le pays du tourisme vrai.* Reprinted by permission of *Office Ivoirien du Tourisme et l'Hôtellerie.*

Using Realia 8-1: La Rentrée des classes

1. **Listening:** Distribute copies of **La Rentrée des classes.** Allow students time to read the text. Then read aloud a series of adjectives (**animé, calme, stressant, tranquille**) and have students tell whether or not each description is appropriate to the setting of the story.

2. **Reading:** Have students read the story and write a summary of the text in three or four sentences.

3. **Reading:** Have students read the biographical information on Bernard Dadié at the bottom of the page. Have them estimate when the story might have taken place. You might have them tell what they think schools in the United States were like during the same time period and how they have changed.

4. **Speaking:** Have students work in pairs. One student should play the role of a student who was at the **rentrée des classes** described in the story. He or she should describe what happened at the **rentrée** in his or her own words. The other student should respond appropriately and ask questions. Then have students change roles.

5. **Writing:** Have students write a letter to a pen pal from Côte d'Ivoire describing what the first day of school was like in their community. Have students ask questions about what the first day of school is like in Côte d'Ivoire in the present day.

6. **Culture:** Have students research schools in Côte d'Ivoire today. You might assign specific questions for students to answer: How many high schools are there in Abidjan? How many students attend each school? What is the average level of education in Côte d'Ivoire? You might also have students find schools from Côte d'Ivoire on the Internet.

Using Realia 8-2: Miss Côte d'Ivoire

1. **Listening:** Divide the class into groups to play a game of Jeopardy®. Read aloud a sentence or part of a sentence from one of Aïcha's answers. (**Je savais que je devais préparer mon baccalauréat.**) Have students tell which question was asked for each response you read.

2. **Reading:** Have students read the interview and underline the information in each of Aïcha's responses that most directly answers the question posed by the magazine. You might have students cross out any information that could be left out of Aïcha's responses without crossing out the answer to the question.

3. **Speaking:** Have students work in pairs to act out an interview. One student should play the role of Aïcha. The other student should interview Aïcha about what life was like when she was younger. Students can base their conversation on the information in the magazine interview and add any details they might want to include.

4. **Speaking:** Have students work in pairs to act out an interview with Aïcha today. The interviewer should ask about Aïcha's past experience as Miss Côte d'Ivoire. The student playing the role of Aïcha should tell what things used to be like when she was Miss Côte d'Ivoire.

R E A L I A

Using Realia: Chapter 8

5. **Writing:** Have students write a short article for a contemporary magazine about Aïcha's life. They could write the article from the point of view of Aïcha or someone else. Students should use the imperfect to describe what things used to be like based on the information in the magazine interview.

6. **Culture:** Have students research the most recent Miss Côte d'Ivoire and gather basic biographical information about her.

Using Realia 8-3: Tours in Côte d'Ivoire

1. **Reading:** Distribute the tour descriptions. Ask students to look at the headings in bold type and to find each region on the map. Then read the tours aloud. Have students trace the tours on their map. Finally, form small groups and have each one read the description of one of the tours and list two or three important features or products of the region.

2. **Speaking:** Have each group in Activity 1 present its findings to the class.

3. **Speaking:** Have students pair off and decide on a region of the country to visit. They should make and reject suggestions and tell why they would choose a certain area before they finally reach a decision.

4. **Speaking:** Have students work in pairs. Have them imagine they are on vacation in Côte d'Ivoire. Have one partner ask the other what type of souvenir he or she would bring for different family members. **(Qu'est-ce que tu vas acheter pour ta tante?)** Have them ask each other where in Côte d'Ivoire they could find the particular item. **(Où est-ce que je peux acheter des tissus?)**

5. **Reading/Listening:** Have students read all the sections in the realia. Read aloud numbered statements and have students try to match each statement with the appropriate region of Côte d'Ivoire. **(1. C'est la région du nord. Elle est célèbre pour le Poro, l'initiation des garçons. 2. C'est une région de grandes forêts,** and so on.)

6. **Writing:** Have students write a short description of a tour in a country of their choice.

7. **Writing:** Tell students to imagine they've just returned from a family stay in Côte d'Ivoire and they're preparing an exhibit of the souvenirs and gifts they brought back with them. They should write a brief description of three items, telling what they are, where they're from, and their significance or purpose.

8. **Culture:** In the information on the Pays Sénoufo, there is a description of **le Poro** (a rite of initiation into manhood). Have groups of students investigate more about this custom in encyclopedias or on the Internet. Then have them present their findings to the class. Have students brainstorm ideas about how our culture celebrates the coming of age. How does a teenager (male or female) know that he or she is seen as an adult in our society?

REALIA

MALADIE D'AMOUR

Realia 9-2

Chère Marjorie

Confiez à Marjorie tous vos problèmes. Elle essaiera de vous comprendre et de vous aider. Marjorie peut trouver une solution à tout!

«Je ne sais pas s'il m'aime vraiment»

Chère Marjorie,

Depuis quatre mois, je sors avec un garçon super. Il a 17 ans. Il est grand, blond et il a les yeux bleus. Toutes mes copines me disent que j'ai beaucoup de chance. Je suis très amoureuse de lui, mais je ne sais pas si lui aussi, il m'aime vraiment. Il ne me dit jamais qu'il m'aime et il sort plus souvent avec ses copains qu'avec moi. Des fois, je ne le vois pas pendant plusieurs jours. Il dit qu'il a trop de choses à faire. Il doit aller chez son cousin, jouer au foot avec son équipe, aller étudier à la bibliothèque ou encore aider un copain avec ses maths. Je ne sais pas si c'est vrai ou bien si ce sont des excuses qu'il invente parce qu'il ne veut pas me voir. Je ne sais plus quoi faire. Donne-moi vite des conseils.

.............................Inès

Inès,

Peut-être que ton petit ami a vraiment beaucoup de choses à faire. Entre le lycée, ses amis, le sport, sa famille et toi, il n'a sûrement pas beaucoup de temps libre. A mon avis, s'il ne voulait pas être avec toi, il aurait cassé. Et puis, votre relation a l'air sérieuse. Vous sortez ensemble depuis quatre mois; c'est beaucoup. Je pense tout simplement qu'il est vraiment très occupé en ce moment. Tu devrais attendre un peu pour voir si les choses s'arrangent. Je suis sûre que bientôt, il aura plus de temps libre pour toi. D'un autre côté, si tu es vraiment triste, tu devrais lui parler. Demande-lui s'il t'aime, s'il est heureux quand il est avec toi. Tout va s'arranger, tu vas voir.

«Je l'aime toujours»

Chère Marjorie,

L'année dernière, je suis sorti avec une fille super, Caroline, pendant deux mois. Tous les garçons du lycée étaient amoureux d'elle et c'est avec moi qu'elle a voulu sortir. J'étais très amoureux d'elle, mais j'ai eu peur qu'elle me quitte pour un autre garçon. Alors, comme je ne voulais pas avoir l'air bête devant tous mes copains, j'ai cassé. Après ça, j'ai déménagé et j'ai changé de lycée. Cette année, je retourne à mon ancien lycée. L'autre jour, j'ai vu Caroline et je crois que je suis toujours amoureux d'elle. J'ai vraiment été stupide de casser. Je voudrais sortir avec elle de nouveau, mais je ne sais pas comment le lui dire. Elle doit sûrement être fâchée contre moi. Qu'est-ce que je peux faire?

.............................Pierrick

Pierrick,

Si tu es vraiment amoureux de Caroline, tu ne devrais pas laisser passer une seconde chance. Ce que tu as fait l'année dernière (casser avec Caroline sans aucune raison) n'était vraiment pas logique. Mais je te comprends. Quand on est amoureux, on fait parfois des choses bizarres. Tu as maintenant l'occasion de tout arranger entre toi et Caroline, alors n'hésite pas. Dis-lui la vérité, explique-lui ce qui s'est passé. A mon avis, elle comprendra. Et puis, bien sûr, dis-lui que tu l'aimes toujours et que tu regrettes ce que tu as fait l'année dernière. Je pense qu'elle te pardonnera. Bon courage!

PETITS MYSTERES

COMMENT NAQUIT LA JEEP?

En un mot, à la faveur de la guerre, la dernière guerre mondiale, s'entend. C'est pour répondre aux besoins de l'armée américaine que Bentam, modeste constructeur, lui présenta en juillet 1940 le projet d'un véhicule tout terrain. Les plans en avaient été ébauchés en cinq jours, et l'on accorda exactement deux mois au fabricant cité pour en livrer le prototype.

L'échéance fut respectée et une première commande expérimentale obtenue. Aucune automobile n'avait encore été dessinée et réalisée à cette vitesse. C'était un exploit. Mais pour le malheur de Bentam, deux concurrents plus gros que lui dépêchèrent des observateurs pour assister aux essais. La loyauté étant le moindre de leurs soucis, il ne leur fallut que quelques jours pour soumettre aux autorités militaires leurs propres modèles, étrangement inspirés. Pouvant offrir des prix plus compétitifs, ils raflèrent le marché. On ne se perdra pas en considérations morales...

Willys seul, puis Ford conjointement, fournirent ainsi à l'armée tous les exemplaires voulus, du véhicule nommé GP pour general purpose (tout usage). Cette abréviation, GP, fut bientôt phonétisée en «Jeep», pour être à présent un nom commun. En 1944, à la libération par les Alliés, les populations européennes s'extasièrent devant l'engin, aussi vif que maniable, qu'était la jeep. Les agriculteurs du monde entier l'utilisent aujourd'hui. Par le manège des consortiums, elle s'est vendue et se vendra sous divers labels, et personne ne s'inquiétera plus de sa paternité.

D'OU L'AMERIQUE TIENT-ELLE SON NOM?

Christophe Colomb, lui, n'a donné le sien qu'à la Colombie. Mais au XVe siècle, il ne fut pas le seul à visiter le Nouveau Monde. Parmi d'autres encore, il y eut Amerigo Vespucci, navigateur florentin - dont un superbe grand voilier italien porte également le nom.

Si Amerigo Vespucci fit plusieurs voyages outre-Atlantique, il les fit après Colomb. Mais le géographe Waldseemüller l'ignorait, et lui attribua à tort la découverte du continent, qu'il baptisa du désormais célèbre prénom. Amerigo Vespucci, pour sa part, n'eut pas le loisir d'en tirer gloriole, pour l'excellente raison qu'il n'en sut jamais rien!

POURQUOI LA TOQUE DES CUISINIERS EST-ELLE SI HAUTE?

Depuis que les gens se font servir à table, donc depuis fort longtemps, ils n'aiment pas trouver de cheveux étrangers dans leur assiette. Si les cuisiniers ont toujours été tenus, ou presque, de se couvrir la tête pour travailler, la toque n'est apparue qu'au XVIIIe siècle. C'est un chef cuisinier de l'Empire qui imagina d'abord, pour ses sous-ordres et lui-même, une coiffe souple en tissu blanc assez ample pour aérer le crâne, lequel transpire abondamment dans la chaleur des fourneaux.

L'exemple fut largement suivi dans les cuisines; mais un peu plus tard, un grand chef viennois, jugeant que ce bonnet informe manquait de majesté, eut l'idée de le redresser en l'armant d'une bande de carton. Maintenant, on empèse les toques à l'amidon, et leur volume doit bien avoir l'efficacité escomptée, puisque personne n'en a encore changé.

QUI A FAIT LE PREMIER SANDWICH?

Nombreux sont les objets baptisés d'après le nom de leur inventeur ou de celui qui en a institué l'usage. C'est le cas, entre autres, de la poubelle, de la montgolfière et de la guillotine. C'est aussi le cas du sandwich, bien que le personnage de ce nom n'ait pas tant fait pour cela que son cuisinier!

Le noble anglais John Montagu, quatrième comte de Sandwich, était un joueur passionné. Un jour de 1762, voyant qu'il refusait tout bonnement de quitter sa table de jeu pour aller dîner, son cuisinier lui fit porter une petite collation improvisée à la hâte. C'était une tranche de viande entre deux tartines de pain beurré.

John Montagu accueillit avec enthousiasme cette innovation qui lui permettrait désormais de prendre ses repas sans s'interrompre dans son activité favorite. La mode du sandwich se répandit alors comme une traînée de poudre à travers les îles britanniques, mais ne gagna les autres pays qu'au siècle suivant. Pour y demeurer, selon toute supposition, aussi longtemps que l'homme ne se nourrira pas de pilules...

"Comment naquit la Jeep?," "D'où l'Amérique tient-elle son nom?," "Pourquoi la toque des cuisiniers est-elle si haute?," and "Qui a fait le premier sandwich?" from "Curiosités: Petits mystères 7" by Frédérique Tugault from *Vidéo-Presse*, vol. XXIV, no. 9. Reprinted by permission of *Copibec*.

REALIA

Using Realia: Chapter 9

Using Realia 9-1: Comic strip

1. **Listening:** Make a transparency and copies of the comic strip. Distribute copies and allow students time to scan the text. Read aloud several true or false descriptions of the characters' feelings as you point out the character you're describing on the transparency: **Elle est amoureuse. (vrai) Il est inquiet. (vrai) Elle est fâchée. (faux)** and so on. Have students call out **vrai** or **faux** according to each description.

2. **Reading:** Ask students a few pre-reading questions before having them read the comic strip closely: What do they expect when reading a comic strip? Are comic strips usually funny? How? After reading, have students report on the subject of the comic strip, whether or not it is realistic or humorous, and why.

3. **Speaking:** Have students work in groups. Students should agree or disagree with the way feelings of love are described in the comic strip and explain why.

4. **Speaking:** Have students conduct a poll of their classmates to see who agrees or disagrees with the way feelings of love are described in the comic strip. Students should divide their data to reflect which answers are given by boys and which by girls. After the whole class has been polled, students should compile the results to see if they reflect the idea in the comic strip that boys and girls probably feel the same when they are in love.

5. **Writing:** Have students imagine and write the dialogue between the two boys in the comic strip which might have led up to what they say in the last frame. Students could write a simple dialogue or create their own comic strips.

6. **Culture:** Have students read the comic strip and underline anything they see in the language that seems different from what they already know about written French. Ask students why they think the language might be presented this way. (It is representative of spoken language.) Have students work in groups to practice reading the dialogue aloud imitating the conversational style of the strip.

Using Realia 9-2: Letters to an advice column

1. **Reading:** Make one copy of the letters for every two students. Cut each paper apart, separating the letters and the replies. Delete the names from each of the letters. Have partners work together to match the letters and the appropriate responses.

2. **Reading:** As a pre-reading activity, ask students what they do when they have a problem and need advice. Distribute the letters. Have students read them and summarize each writer's problem and Marjorie's advice.

3. **Reading:** Prepare in advance a series of questions targeting specific information presented in the letters. **(Quel âge a le petit ami d'Inès?)** Distribute copies of the letters and allow students enough time to read them once, before you start asking the questions.

4. **Listening:** Prepare a list of true-false statements. **(Le petit ami d'Inès a 25 ans.)** Distribute copies of the letters and allow students enough time to read them. Then tell students to raise their right hands when they hear a true statement and to raise their left hands when they hear a false statement.

5. **Listening:** Quote from the letters at random and have students identify the writer.

6. **Speaking:** Have partners create a conversation in which one person has a problem and asks for advice. The other partner should express sympathy and offer some advice.

7. **Writing:** Have students write their own response to one of the letters in **Chère Marjorie.**

Using Realia 9-3: How common items came into existence

1. **Reading:** As a pre-reading activity, ask students if they know the origin of any very common objects or names, such as they might read in *Ripley's Believe It or Not.* Distribute the articles. Assign each article to a group of students. They should summarize it and report their findings to the class.

2. **Listening:** Make true-false statements about the objects or names described in the articles. Students should make a thumbs-up signal to indicate a true statement or a thumbs-down signal to indicate a false statement. You may want to have students correct the false statements. **Ford a fait le premier prototype de la Jeep. (faux) Amerigo Vespucci a visité le Nouveau Monde après Christophe Colomb. (vrai)**

3. **Speaking:** Have partners take turns telling each other the origin of one of the objects or names. They might ask questions of each other as they listen.

4. **Speaking:** Divide the class into groups. Assign one article to each of the groups. Then have each group tell the story from their article to another group with each student contributing a part of the story. They should continue telling the story until the other group guesses which article they have. Have groups take turns telling their stories. Have each group describe their article for at least two other groups.

5. **Writing:** Have students research the origin of a common object of their choice and write a description of its history. Students might compile their descriptions into an article to be distributed to other French classes or sent to pen pals.

6. **Culture:** Have students research the origin of objects that are historically linked or associated with France. You might suggest the 2CV car by Citroën, high-heeled shoes, the baguette, the Eiffel Tower, the Concorde, pasteurization, radium, the TGV, and so on.

R E A L I A

Realia 10-1

QUELQUES CONSEILS POUR SE FAIRE DES AMIS

AIMEZ-VOUS ET RESPECTEZ-VOUS

Avant de pouvoir avoir des amis qui vous apprécient sincèrement, il faut apprendre à vous aimer vous-même, physiquement et morale-ment. C'est la base de toute communication. Comment faire? C'est très simple. Si vous donnez aux autres l'image d'une personne confiante, heureuse et bien dans sa peau, tout le monde voudra mieux vous connaître et vous aurez des tas d'amis. Pour commencer, mettez en valeur vos qualités et vos points forts. Ensuite, travaillez sur vos points faibles et surtout, ne cessez jamais de croire en vous-même. Si vous ne réussissez pas à faire quelque chose de façon parfaite, persévérez. Essayez de faire de votre mieux; c'est ça qui compte. Ne vous découragez pas. Et puis, si ce n'est vraiment pas votre truc, ce n'est pas grave. Après tout, vous êtes sûre-ment très doué pour autre chose. Tout le monde ne peut pas être bon à tout. L'essentiel, c'est de rester positif, le reste suivra.

APPRENEZ A ECOUTER LES AUTRES

Vos amis jouent un rôle très important dans votre vie. Vous partagez tout. A part votre famille, c'est avec eux que vous passez le plus de temps. Vous discutez, vous vous amusez, vous faites la fête ensemble... Dans les moments de joie, ils sont toujours là. Mais les vrais amis sont aussi là quand vous avez besoin d'eux, dans les moments de doute ou de tristesse. Ils vous écoutent, vous aident à résoudre vos problèmes. Ils vous réconfortent quand vous en avez besoin. Vous aussi, vous devez être prêt à faire des sacrifices pour vos amis. Vous devez être compréhensif et attentif à leurs problèmes. Vous devez être capable de sentir quand quelque chose ne va pas. Vous devez les écouter et leur offrir des conseils. Après tout, tout le monde sait qu'il est bien plus facile de

résoudre les problèmes des autres que les siens. Si vous voulez que votre amitié dure, répondez à l'appel de vos amis quand ils ont besoin de vous, pas seulement quand tout va bien.

N'HESITEZ PAS A FAIRE LE PREMIER PAS

Chaque fois que vous avez l'occa-sion de vous faire de nouveaux amis, n'hésitez pas. Ne jugez pas les gens sur leur apparence. Ce n'est pas parce que quelqu'un a l'air froid et distant qu'il l'est réellement. Peut-être que cette personne est tout simplement timide. Alors, donnez la même chance à tout le monde. Il est possible que quelqu'un qui, au départ, vous paraissait peu sympa-thique devienne par la suite votre meilleur ami. Ne jugez pas non plus les gens sur les vêtements qu'ils portent ou sur leur coupe de cheveux. Nous avons tous des goûts différents en ce qui concerne la mode et ce serait très superficiel de juger une personne d'après ce qu'elle porte. Vous n'aimeriez sans doute pas qu'on vous juge aussi rapidement sans même vous con-naître, alors ne le faites pas non plus.

SOYEZ OUVERT

Il est important, quand on veut garder ses amis, d'être ouvert. Etre ouvert, c'est aimer beaucoup de choses, c'est vouloir essayer de nou-velles activités ou de nouveaux sports. C'est aussi aimer sortir, que ce soit aller au musée, au cinéma ou encore au restaurant. Plus vous vous intéresserez à beaucoup de choses, plus vous rencontrerez des gens in-

téressants avec qui vous pour-rez devenir amis. Alors, n'hésitez pas. Inscrivez-vous dans de nombreux clubs tels que clubs de sports, de théâtre, de photographie, Maison des jeu-nes et de la culture... où vous pour-rez appren-dre toutes sortes de choses passionnantes tout en rencontrant de nombreux jeunes qui partagent vos goûts et vos in-térêts.

AYEZ UN BON SENS DE L'HUMOUR

L'humour est quelque chose de très important dans toutes rela-tions avec autrui. Si vous savez rire et faire rire, vous serez populaire avec tout le monde. Bien sûr, il faut aussi savoir où s'arrêter et parfois, les blagues les plus courtes sont les meilleures. Vos amis apprécieront votre humour encore plus si vous savez aussi être sérieux quand il le faut.

BOUGEZ!

Soyez dynamique! Plus vous aurez d'énergie et plus vous aurez envie de faire des choses, plus on vous admirera. Ne restez pas seul dans votre coin à vous plaindre de tout. Ne vous enfermez pas chez vous dès que quelque chose ne va pas. Ce n'est pas la meilleure façon de se faire des amis. Au contraire, sortez, bougez. Si vous êtes plein d'enthousiasme et si vous êtes tou-jours prêt à agir, vous deviendrez très vite le leader de votre groupe d'amis et vous serez un exemple pour les plus timides.

PRENEZ SOIN DE VOUS

Certes, il ne faut pas juger les gens sur leur apparence. Mais d'un autre côté, nous avons tous ten-

dance à aller plus facilement vers les gens qui nous paraissent sympa ou cool. Alors, ne vous négligez pas. Mettez vos qualités en valeur, portez des vêtements qui vous vont bien, des couleurs agréables. Souriez, soyez aimable avec les gens et vous verrez qu'eux aussi, ils seront plus sympathiques avec vous.

FAITES PREUVE DE PERSONNALITE

Ne vous laissez pas influencer et n'essayez pas de faire plaisir à tout le monde. N'abandonnez jamais vos principes parce qu'ils déplaisent à certains. Vos goûts, vos ambitions, vos opinions, vos valeurs morales sont peut-être totalement différents de ceux de quelqu'un d'autre, mais cela ne prouve pas que vous avez tort et que l'autre a raison. De votre côté, n'essayez pas d'imposer votre façon de voir les choses aux autres. L'intolérance est un sérieux défaut dont il est néces-saire de se débarrasser si on veut réussir à se faire des amis.

SACHEZ CONSERVER VOS AMITIES

Faites un effort pour garder vos amis. En effet, s'il est assez facile de se faire des amis, il est beaucoup plus difficile de les conserver. Alors, soyez patient, compréhensif et franc. N'oubliez pas que l'honnêteté marche à tous les coups alors que l'hypocrisie, la jalousie, l'égoïsme et les petites mesquineries ne vous apporteront que des déceptions.

Faites la fête!

La fin de l'année scolaire approche. Ça se fête!

L'invitation

Lancez l'invitation 3 semaines à l'avance. Vous ne pourrez sûrement pas vous empêcher d'annoncer bien fort votre projet aux intéressés, mais une carte sera quand même bienvenue! Précisez l'heure de début et de fin, au moins on sera fixé pour les accompagnements et les raccompagnements.

La préparation

Prévoyez à l'avance comment vous nourrirez la horde affamée qui s'annonce. Faites, si possible, tous les achats l'avant-veille. La veille et le jour même, vous n'aurez plus qu'à découper, mixer, tartiner... Mettez-vous d'accord avec vos parents : de quelle manière ils seront sur place (question de sécurité), quels meubles vous allez déplacer pour avoir un espace-danse (terriblement lourd, ce canapé...), quels objets délicats sont à déménager d'urgence (pas touche à la porcelaine de Tatie Georgina!). Si les voisins risquent de constater une légère augmentation du niveau sonore environnant, prévenez-les par une petite carte l'avant-veille. Ils pourront organiser un repli chez les amis si nécessaire.

Le buffet

Le mieux est de dresser deux buffets, en proposant les mêmes choses en même temps sur les deux. Le salé a toujours du succès. Pour tout préparer, demander un coup de main à votre meilleur(e) ami(e), ce sera plus drôle! Prévoyez plusieurs boissons : du soda, bien sûr, mais aussi différents jus de fruits, gazeux et non-gazeux, et de l'eau. Marquez les verres : sur du plastique, le feutre indélébile marche très bien. Vive les assiettes et gobelets en carton! Coordonnez leurs couleurs au décor, ou au contraire imaginez des oppositions qui flashent.

La musique

La musique est le cœur d'une fête. Variez les styles, rock, dance ou rap, pimentez de-ci, de-là avec un bon vieux tube des années 60. Pourquoi ne pas demander à vos amis un de leurs disques préférés (marqué à leur nom!) Prévoyez une bonne sono, en faisant des essaies pour repartir les baffles. Réglez-les à un niveau supportable pour l'oreille humaine... L'idéal, c'est quelqu'un qui ne s'occupe que de la musique : si vous avez un copain ou un grand frère qui accepte de faire le disc-jockey, ce sera le luxe.

L'ambiance

C'est l'affaire de tous, mais celui qui invite a un rôle irremplaçable. À lui de faire que tout le monde se sente à l'aise. De veiller à ce que personne ne se sente mis à l'écart. Si l'un d'entre vous est un animateur-né, il peut lancer un concours de danse, des imitations, un karaoké... Les talents de vos invités vont se révéler, et vous passerez tous ensemble le moment le plus sympa de l'année. Alors très, très bonne fête!

Texte : Monique Scherrer   Illustrations : David Scrima

Realia 10-3

REALIA

l'amitié
sans limites

Les amis, c'est sacré. On ferait tout pour eux. Tout. Pourtant, quelquefois, on se rend compte qu'on n'a pas tout fait... qu'il aurait mieux valu en faire un peu moins... ou pas comme ça...

Le mot le plus cruel en amitié, c'est trahison. La grande trahison, c'est de laisser tomber un ami parce qu'on en a trouvé un autre plus intéressant. C'est vrai que les amitiés évoluent avec le temps, parce que nous changeons tous, nous et nos amis. Si on n'a plus de plaisir à être ensemble et à partager, c'est qu'il n'y a plus d'amitié entre nous. Ce n'est pas une trahison de s'éloigner l'un de l'autre à ce moment-là. C'est même une bonne chose. Mais si un ami avec qui on partageait tout jusqu'à hier encore, ne veut plus nous voir du tout parce qu'il a rencontré un autre ami, là, celui qui est abandonné le ressent comme une trahison. Il ne compte plus, il n'existe plus aux yeux de l'autre. C'est une grande souffrance...

Heureusement, les grandes trahisons sont rares.

Trahison rime aussi avec pardon

Une trahison bien visible, c'est un ami qui répète les confidences qu'on lui a faites à tous les copains, pour faire rire les autres, ou pour se faire bien voir... Ou alors, on répète, mais sous le sceau du secret : *"Julie, tu me jures de pas répéter, mais tu sais, Julien patati patata"* et le jour même Julie fait jurer à Amélie de ne pas le répéter... Ça circule très vite, ce genre de propos.

Et les trahisons silencieuses? Lorsque dans un groupe, tous rigolent en entendant Jérémie raconter *"comment c'est nul la pièce qu'ils jouent à l'atelier théâtre, surtout Fabrice qui a l'air débile"*, le meilleur ami de Fabrice s'il ne dit rien, il le trahit, sans rien dire, "sans faire exprès"... C'est vrai, ce n'est pas facile d'affronter tout un groupe pour défendre son ami. Alors qu'il est si facile de faire rire aux dépens des autres...

Mais trahison, ça rime aussi avec pardon. Souvent, le plus difficile, ce n'est pas d'accorder son pardon, mais d'oser le demander. Si on tient vraiment à une amitié, il faut trouver le courage de le faire.

Chacun son genre et son style. On peut téléphoner, écrire un petit mot, le faire avec humour... les grandes scènes tragiques ne sont pas indispensables.

Aimer vraiment quelqu'un, pour lui

Pas facile, mais quand l'ami fâché vous regarde en souriant à nouveau, quel bonheur!

From "L'amitié sans limites" from *Okapi*, no. 602. Copyright © by **Bayard Presse International**. Reprinted by permission of the publisher.

Using Realia 10-1: Tips for making friends

1. **Reading/Writing:** Distribute the tips for making friends. Ask students to skim the advice given in the bold-faced subheadings under numbers 1 to 9. Have them rank the advice from most to least meaningful. Then have groups of students read an assigned section of the tips, write out a statement of the main idea, and report it to the class.

2. **Listening:** Make random statements of advice from the various sections and have students identify the appropriate section.

3. **Listening:** Make random statements about problems teenagers have. Students should identify the section that suggests appropriate advice.

4. **Speaking:** Have partners create a conversation in which a student asks a friend, teacher, or parent for advice on making friends.

5. **Writing:** Have students write a fictitious letter to an advice column in which they explain why they don't have many friends. Then have them exchange letters and write a response.

6. **Writing:** Have students make a list of ten things they shouldn't do if they want to make friends.

Using Realia 10-2: How to plan a party

1. **Listening:** Distribute copies of the article on planning a party and allow students time to scan the text. Then describe several activities that you do to prepare a party. Have students tell what category the activity you describe falls under: **l'invitation, la préparation, le buffet,** and so on.

2. **Reading:** Divide students into five groups, one for each stage of planning a party, according to the article. Then have each group read the information and organize a list of responsibilities for the activities in their assigned section. For example, the group that works with **L'invitation** should choose a party date, time, and location, design invitations, specify who will send the invitations and on what day. Students could present their activities to the class for performance assessment or submit their written work to be included in a portfolio.

3. **Speaking:** Have students work in groups to organize a party. Students should designate exactly what they need to do, based on the article. Then students should discuss who in their group will do which activities on their list of preparations until they feel that the entire party is organized.

4. **Writing:** Have students write notes to a few different people asking for help with planning an upcoming party. Each student should write one note to his or her parent to get permission for the party, a second note to his or her best friend to get help making the food preparations, and a third note to a brother or sister to get their assistance in organizing the music for their party. Students may write more notes if they wish.

Using Realia: Chapter 10

5. **Culture:** Have students research when the school year typically begins and ends in France. Have them compare their findings to their own school calendar and any differences there might be in choosing a date for an end-of-the-school-year party.

Using Realia 10-3: Friendship

1. **Listening:** Write the words **trahison** and **pardon** on the board. Then read aloud some of the functions from the third **étape**. (**Désolé. C'est de ma faute. Ça ne fait rien. C'est pas grave.**) Have students indicate whether the statements you read would be more appropriate to apologize for betraying a friend **(trahison)** or to accept an apology **(pardon)**.

2. **Reading:** Have students read the article to find specific examples of situations where one friend hurts another's feelings.

3. **Speaking:** Using the information they gathered from the reading activity, have students act out dialogues where one student apologizes for hurting his or her friend's feelings. The other student should reproach his or her partner before accepting the apology.

4. **Writing:** Have students write a note to a friend to apologize for hurting his or her feelings. Students should explain what they did and offer some reproach for their actions (**j'aurais dû... , j'aurais pu...**). You might have partners exchange letters and write notes accepting the apology of their partner.

5. **Culture:** Point out to students the use of the expression **patati patata** in the article. Have students give the equivalent expression or expressions in English.

REALIA

French 2 Allez, viens!, Chapter 10

musique

Bouge ta tête

Jamiroquai explosif

Jamiroquai conjugue funk, soul et acid jazz. Son chanteur, Jason Kay, se distingue par sa voix et sa personnalité fantastique. Leurs deux premiers albums

viennent d'être réédités. Bon plan!
Emergency On Planet Earth et *The Return Of The Space Cowboy.* Small/Sony

U2 animé

Après Aerosmith, U2 a accepté de figurer dans un épisode du dessin animé *Les Simpsons.* Y a pas que Bart qui va être content!

Les Poetic Lover
soul et R&B

Les Poetic Lover se sont connus au lycée. Alors que le rap y règne en maître, eux préfèrent les beats R&B et les mélodies soul. Si le succès les a déjà rattrapés, ils continuent d'habiter chez leurs parents. "Nous venons d'un milieu modeste et nous connaissons la valeur des choses."
Amants Poétiques, Poetic Lover. M6/Sony

Incroyable!
Vanessa Mae
La pop classique

A une année lumière des Boys ou Girls Bands qui vivent un succès pas toujours mérité, Vanessa Mae récolte les lauriers d'années de labeur. Née un 27 octobre à Singapour, elle commence ses études de piano et de violon dès 4 ans. A 10 ans, elle donne son premier concert symphonique et à 12, elle part pour sa première tournée internationale. Elle sera rapidement reconnue comme la plus jeune interprète à avoir enregistré les concerts pour violon de Tchaikovsky et Beethoven! Le début d'une grande carrière classique? Pas seulement, puisqu'à 14 ans, elle décide d'écrire pour le violon acoustique mais aussi électrique. Aujourd'hui, elle signe des albums qui mélangent virtuosité classique, légèreté pop, énergie rock. Cette fan de Bob Marley triture son Stradivarius comme personne. A 18 ans, elle a déjà vendu plus de 3 millions de disques. *Storm* Odéon/EMI

Elle a plus d'une corde à son archet...

Concours Okapi-Vercoquin

Nouveaux venus sur la scène pop française, les Vercoquin laissent libre cours à leurs tendances grunge et funk. Pour les découvrir, c'est facile : Adresse une carte postale à Concours Okapi-Vercoquin, Cedex 2720, 99272 Paris Concours. En indiquant tes nom, âge et adresse. *Vercoquin.* Island

From "Musique" from *Okapi,* no. 622. Copyright © by **Bayard Presse International.** Reprinted by permission of the publisher.

Realia 11-2

CHOUANS! - Français, couleurs. Fresque historique de Philippe de Broca : Pendant la Terreur, Chouans et Révolutionnaires se livrent une guerre sans merci. Deux frères de lait, épris de la même femme, se retrouvent dans les camps adverses. Avec Philippe Noiret, Sophie Marceau, Lambert Wilson.

INDISCRETIONS (The Philadelphia Story) - Américain, noir et blanc. (40). Comédie de George Cukor : Une séparation fracassante suivie d'une réconciliation non moins inattendue! Un pur chef-d'œuvre de la comédie américaine. Avec Cary Grant, Katharine Hepburn, James Stewart. (vo).

CARAVAGGIO - Britannique, couleurs. Biographie de Derek Jarman : La vie du célèbre peintre italien. Sa liaison avec un joueur vénal et son épouse. Avec Dexter Fletcher, Sean Bean, Tilda Swinton, Michael Gough, Nigel Davenport, Robbie Coltrane, Jonathan Hyde. (vo).

CHAMBRE AVEC VUE - Britannique, couleurs. Comédie dramatique de James Ivory : Au début du siècle, à Florence, une jeune Anglaise très «comme il faut» s'éprend d'un concitoyen peu conventionnel. Son chaperon décide de rentrer en Angleterre... D'après Forster. Avec Maggie Smith, Helena Bonham Carter, Denholm Eliott, Julian Sands, Daniel Day Lewis, Simon Callow. (vo).

LONGUE VIE A LA SIGNORA - Italien, couleurs. Comédie dramatique de Ermanno Olmi : Un adolescent fait

Les Fiches de plus de
10 000 FILMS
dont les plus importants et tous les nouveaux films sortis à Paris depuis 1973
(complément des années antérieures en cours de saisie)
Sélections simples ou croisées par
titre (v.f. ou v.o.), interprète, réalisateur, année, pays, genre
C'est le Répertoire Films sur minitel

ses débuts de serveur dans un hôtel de luxe. D'abord émerveillé, il perçoit bientôt la dureté de l'existence. Avec Marco Esposito, Simona Brandalise. (vf).

JEAN DE FLORETTE - Français, couleurs. Drame paysan de Claude Berri : Un garçon de la ville hérite d'une propriété en Provence. Deux voisins, par cupidité, lui cachent l'existence d'une source, compromettant ainsi ses efforts. D'après Marcel Pagnol. Avec Yves Montand, Gérard Depardieu, Daniel Auteuil.

CAMOMILLE - Français, couleurs. Comédie dramatique de Mehdi Charef : La rencontre insolite d'un garçon boulanger et d'une fille de famille fortunée, à qui l'amour fait cruellement défaut. Avec Philippine Leroy-Beaulieu, Rémi Martin, Monique Chaumette, Guy Saint-Jean, Albert Delphy, Michel Peyrelon.

YEUX NOIRS (LES) (Oci ciornie) - Italien, couleurs. Comédie dramatique de Nikita Mikhalkov : Au début de ce siècle, un Italien poursuit jusqu'en Russie la femme qu'il aime. De retour, il n'ose avouer la vérité à son épouse. D'après Anton Tchekhov. Avec Marcello Mastroianni, Elena Sofonova. (vo).

TERRE DE FER, CIEL DE CUIVRE - Germano-turc, couleurs. Comédie dramatique de Omer Zülfü Livaneli : Dans un petit village d'Anatolie, un homme qui tente de déjouer les intrigues du maire passe pour un Saint. Bientôt, il se voit assailli par les malades et les infirmes. Avec Rutkay Aziz, Yavuzer Cetinkaya, Macide Tanir, Eray Ozbal, Serap Aksoy. (vo).

ASTERIX CHEZ LES BRETONS - Français, couleurs. Dessin animé de Pino van Lawsweerde : Astérix et ses compagnons, en volant au secours d'un village breton menacé par les Romains, se laissent ravir le précieux tonneau contenant leur potion magique.

AU REVOIR LES ENFANTS - Franco-allemand, couleurs. Drame de Louis Malle : En 1944, un jeune Israélite trouve refuge dans une pension religieuse. Il se lie d'amitié avec l'un

de ses compagnons. Mais une dénonciation le perdra. Lion d'or Venise. Avec Gaspard Manesse, Raphaël Fetjö, Francine Racette.

CANDY MOUNTAIN - Américano-canadien, couleurs. Comédie dramatique de Robert Frank et Rudy Wurlitzer : L'errance et la quête initiatique d'un jeune musicien de rock à la recherche d'un légendaire fabricant de guitares. Entre Jim Jarmusch et Jack Kerouac. Avec Kevin O'Connor, Harris Yulin, Tom Waits. (vf).

TAMPOPO - Japonais, couleurs. Comédie de Juzo Itami : La restauratrice Tampopo supplie un routier fin gourmet de lui enseigner l'art de cuisiner. Une façon de démontrer que les Japonais ne pensent pas qu'au travail! Avec Nobuko Miyamoto, Tsutomu Yamazaki, Ken Watanabe, Rikiya Yasuoka, Koji Yakusho, Fukumi Kuroda. (vo).

DERNIER EMPEREUR (LE) - Italo-britannique, couleurs. Fresque historique de Bernardo Bertolucci : La vie du dernier Empereur de Chine, Pu Yi, promu à 3 ans, puis chassé de Pékin, arrêté par les Russes en 1945, remis à la Chine en 50 et libéré 10 ans plus tard au terme d'une longue «rééducation». Avec John Lone, Peter O'Toole, Joan Chen, Ying Ruovcheng, Victor Wong, Dennis Dun, Ryuichi Sakamoto, Wu Jun Mei. (vo).

VIE EST UN LONG FLEUVE TRANQUILLE (LA) - Français, couleurs. Comédie d'Etienne Chatiliez : Par dépit amoureux, une infirmière a échangé deux nouveaux-nés : l'un d'une famille bourgeoise, l'autre de sous-prolos. Le «scandale» éclate un jour! Avec Daniel Gélin, Hélène Vincent, André Wilms, Catherine Hiegel, Maurice Mons, Christine Pignet, Catherine Jacob, Patrick Bouchitey.

TINTIN ET LE TEMPLE DU SOLEIL - Franco-belge, couleurs. Dessin animé de Raymond Leblanc : Tintin et ses amis partent à la recherche du Professeur Tournesol, enlevé pour avoir profané une momie Inca. D'après la B.D. d'Hergé.

livres

Meurtres à 30 000 km/s

A bord du *Space Beagle II*, le fabuleux vaisseau spatial qui rentre d'une mission scientifique, il se passe des choses terribles. Les membres de l'équipage sont victimes de meurtres atroces. La jeune Alex se lance sur la piste des assassins, aidée de Puck, son fidèle robot : "personnalité unique à circuits kryptonisés." Monte, toi aussi, dans le *Space Beagle*, mais attention, le voyage sera mouvementé!

Meurtres à 30 000 km/s, de Christophe Lambert, Hachette jeunesse, Science-Fiction, 190 p, 4,20 €

Dis-moi tout!

Wladys cache une blessure secrète. Anne l'aime beaucoup et veut découvrir son secret. Son chemin vers le cœur de son ami sera parsemé de questions et d'émotion. Suis-la.

Dis-moi tout! de Marie Desplechin, coll. Je Bouquine Envol, Bayard Poche, 91 p, 4,20 €

Déchets
la planète en péril

Pour tout savoir sur le casse-tête des déchets : leur histoire, leurs dangers, leurs traitements. Plonge-toi dans ce petit livre habile et passionnant, de la taille d'un CD. Bourré d'infos!

Déchets, la planète en péril, de Sylvia Vaisman, Les compacts de l'info, Casterman, 48 p, 4,40 €

La bande dessinée
Trent : le pays sans soleil

Imagine-toi vivant au nord du cercle polaire, complètement seul dans une cabane perdue dans la neige, le froid et la nuit. C'est ce qui arrive au sergent Trent, de la police montée canadienne, qui attend la relève dans cet enfer désert et gelé. Mais une nuit, Trent découvre un enfant, blanc, braillant à côté d'une indienne morte de froid... Quel est ce mystère? Avec ce western, pas de bagarres, de galopades et de fusillades, mais beaucoup d'émotion.

Scénario de Rodolphe, dessins de Léo, Dargaud, 8 €

Ne rate pas le début
Max, mon frère

"**T**u mens! ai-je crié, furieuse. Tu mens comme tu respires! N'importe qui voit bien que j'ai plus de taches de rousseur que toi. Ouvre donc les yeux espèce de taupe! Max, allongé sur le sable, souriait ironiquement.
—Tu t'es bien défoulée, ma grosse? a-t-il demandé, l'air de s'ennuyer profondément.

J'ai senti le rouge me monter au visage. J'ai respiré un grand coup, et j'ai sauté sur la forteresse de sable qu'on venait de construire ensemble. Puis je me suis enfuie en courant aussi vite que j'ai pu. Quand j'ai été certaine qu'il ne me poursuivait pas, je me suis mise à pester tout haut, tout en ralentissant. Une taupe, qu'il était! Parfaitement! Et vache en plus de ça! Ah, si on avait pu me donner un autre frère! J'en avais vraiment assez, de celui-là. Cela durait depuis dix ans. Et même depuis beaucoup plus longtemps, puisqu'on était déjà ensemble dans le ventre de Maman. Je n'y pouvais rien si on était jumeaux! Et Max était certainement aussi vache en ce temps-là. Et puis il m'appelait tout le temps "sa grosse". Quand j'étais petite, j'étais un peu ronde, mais depuis le temps, comme disait Maman, j'avais bien fondu. Décidément, Max était une taupe! Je me suis laissée tomber sur la plage et j'ai regardé autour de moi. Beaucoup de gens se prélassaient au soleil. La plupart luisaient tellement ils s'étaient enduits de graisse. ●●●

Si tu veux connaître la suite, cours vite chez ton libraire!

Max, mon frère, de Sigrid Zeevaert, Bayard Poche, coll. Je Bouquine Envol, 93 p, 4,20 €

Using Realia: Chapter 11

Using Realia 11-1: Music reviews

1. **Reading:** Distribute copies of the music reviews and have students look for information in each review that tells what kind of music the musician(s) perform.

2. **Listening:** Have students scan the music reviews. Then read aloud a series of true-false statements about the musicians described. (**Jamiroquai est un chanteur. Vanessa Mae joue du piano,** and so on.) Have students tell whether each statement is true or false and have them correct false statements.

3. **Speaking:** Have students work in pairs. Assign or have students choose one of the artists from the music reviews. Each student should read the review for his or her artist. Then have partners act out a conversation between an employee and a customer at a music store. The employee should recommend to the customer the music he or she read about, describing the type of music based on the information in the review. The customer should decide whether or not to buy a CD according to the recommendation. Then partners should change roles.

4. **Writing:** Have students write a review in French of one of their favorite CDs, musicians, or bands. Students should describe where the musician or band is from and what kind of music they play. Students should model their reviews on the magazine's music reviews.

5. **Writing:** Have students write a letter to a French-speaking pen pal recommending some music they recently purchased. They should pick one of the musical groups or musicians from the reviews and describe the music to their pen pal.

Using Realia 11-2: Movie listings

1. **Reading:** As a pre-reading activity, have students list the kinds of information they would expect to find in a movie listing. Distribute the movie listings. Have students scan the listings, comparing their expectations with the types of information included. Assign groups of students a section of the realia. Have them verify that their list matches the information presented.

2. **Reading:** Have students read through the listings and categorize the various movies according to genre (**film comique, film d'horreur,** and so on).

3. **Listening:** Read aloud the descriptions of various movies and have students identify the types of movies you're describing.

4. **Listening:** Read aloud one or two details pertaining to a particular movie and have students identify the movie to which you are referring. (**C'est un drame avec Yves Montand. C'est un film de Claude Berri.**) *(Jean de Florette)*

5. **Speaking:** Have partners act out a conversation in which one person invites the other to go to the movies. They discuss the types of movies each person would like to see. Finally, they agree on one of the movies shown in the movie listings.

French 2 Allez, viens!, Chapter 11

REALIA

6. **Speaking:** Have partners act out a conversation between two movie critics. The partners should give their opinions of various movies, identify the movie type, describe the plots, and either recommend them or discourage the public from seeing them.

7. **Writing:** Have students write a brief description of a movie of their choice. Have them model their description after the movie listings on the realia page. You might have students form groups after they each write a description. They could put their descriptions together and create their own movie listings page.

8. **Writing:** Have students write a short letter telling their best friend about a movie they want to see. They should choose one of the movies from the listings. Have them describe the movie to their friend and explain why they recommend the film.

9. **Culture:** *Jean de Florette* and *Au revoir les enfants* are considered classics of French cinema. Have students choose one of these films and find out as much as possible about the filmmaker, actors, plot, and so on. Have students present their findings to the class. You might consider previewing one of the films and showing it or excerpts from it in class.

Using Realia 11-3: Book reviews

1. **Listening:** Distribute copies of the book reviews and allow students time to read through the descriptions of each book. Then read aloud short descriptions of each book in which you give an opinion and summarize the story. Have students name the book that you're describing.

2. **Reading:** Have students read through the book reviews and give an opinion of each book based on the review.

3. **Speaking:** Have students work in pairs to act out a conversation between a customer and a bookstore employee. The customer should ask for recommendations about what to buy. Then the employee should suggest one or two of the books from the book reviews, summarizing the plot of each book and giving a favorable opinion. Have students change roles.

4. **Writing:** Have students work in groups to create a book review page for a magazine or newspaper. Students should write reviews in French of their favorite book or books, including the type of book, a summary of the plot, and an opinion of the book. Students can then design a page for their book reviews using posterboard and including drawings or other art to illustrate their reviews.

5. **Culture:** Give students a list of well-known French authors or book titles. Have students pick an author or title. The students should research the author, genre, plot, and length of a particular title, or basic biographical facts and well-known titles written by a particular author.

R E A L I A

CAMP DE JEUNES
15-18 ans

DÉBUTANT ou CONFIRMÉ

LA CROISIÈRE

Navigation sur voilier de 10,50 à 11 m sous la responsabilité d'un chef de bord. Périmètre de navigation de Camaret à l'île d'Yeu. Couchage sur le bateau - Possibilité de navigation vers la Bretagne nord (séjour de 2 semaines). Programme : Conduite du voilier, manœuvres, lecture de carte et compas, organisation de la vie à bord, les marées, phares, balisage...

L'ACTIVITÉ VOILE

1 ou 2 activités voile suivant les séjours à choisir dans les activités de l'école de voile ci-contre (dériveur, planche à voile, catamaran).

LE GOLF

Activité golf avec club du Croisic sous la conduite d'un moniteur diplômé, apprentissage sur practice puis parcours de 2 heures par jour.

L'HÉBERGEMENT

L'hébergement durant la semaine de camp à terre se déroule sous tente dans l'enceinte du CENTRE MARCEAU sur la plage Valentin. Tous les repas sont pris au centre, dans la salle à manger.

CAMPS DE JEUNES

"VOILE À GOGO"

CROISIÈRE, VOILE, GOLF
1ère SEMAINE : CROISIÈRE
2e SEMAINE : CAMP A TERRE
VOILE 1/2 JOURNÉE
GOLF 1/2 JOURNÉE

	PRIX	CODE
du 12 au 25 JUILLET	600	CJ1

CROISIÈRE, VOILE (2 ACTIVITÉS)
1ère SEMAINE : CROISIÈRE
2e SEMAINE : CAMP A TERRE
VOILE LE MATIN
ET L'APRÈS-MIDI

	PRIX	CODE
du 1 au 14 AOÛT	600	CJ2
du 16 au 29 AOÛT	600	CJ3

CAMP

"CROISIÈRE À GOGO"

1 SEMAINE	PRIX	CODE
du 12 au 18 JUILLET	300	CC1
du 26 JUILLET au 1 AOÛT	285	CC4
du 2 au 8 AOÛT	300	CC6
du 23 au 29 AOÛT	300	CC7
du 30 AOÛT au 5 SEPT.	285	CC3

2 SEMAINES	PRIX	CODE
du 19 JUILLET au 1 AOÛT	595	CC2
du 9 au 22 AOÛT	595	CC5

Les prix s'entendent tout compris : activités, prêt combinaison (PAV), frais de port, nourriture, assurance, matériel golf, séjour agréé jeunesse et sports, bons CAF acceptés

CENTRE DE VACANCES 6-13 ANS

Séjour de 2-3 ou 4 semaines durant les mois de juillet-août et les vacances de Pâques :
Activités voile, plage, tir à l'arc...
Coût et dates : se renseigner
Hébergement dans le centre Marceau situé au bord de la mer, sur la plage Valentin.

CLASSES DE DÉCOUVERTES - GROUPES

De mars à octobre et depuis 1974, nous accueillons des classes de découvertes mer. Forts de notre expérience et du cadre de découverte très riche, les enfants et leurs enseignants disposent de tous les éléments pour une vraie "classe de découverte". Personnel qualifié. Hébergement dans le centre Marceau.

PÉRIODE SCOLAIRE

— Activité voile avec les enfants des écoles de la presqu'île
— Accueil de groupes et collèges

FORMATION MONITEURS DE VOILE FFV

— Stage BO : Aide moniteur : sur demande (juillet-août)
— Stage A2C1 : Acquisition niveau théorique et pratique DER, PAV, KATA du 25 avril au 1 mai et du 18 avril au 24 avril   Coût : 275 €
— Stage B1 Pédagogique du 29/08 au 6/09   Coût : 395 €

DANS UN CADRE EXCEPTIONNEL

HÉBERGEMENT

Dans un centre de qualité, le centre Marceau : salle d'activité, réfectoire, chambre de 4, parc boisé, plage à 10 m., bibliothèque, 90 lits, entièrement rénové.

Le centre Marceau est situé sur la plage Valentin au bord de l'océan, à 100 m des marais salants de Batz, à 1 km du terminus TGV, à 2 km du port de pêche du Croisic et de son océarium.

CONDITIONS D'INSCRIPTION

— Remplir le bulletin d'inscription;
— Joindre 30 € d'arrhes par stage (stage external) ou 150 € d'arrhes (stage internat);
— Règlement par chèque C.C.P. ou Chèque Bancaire à l'ordre de "**École de Voile Valentin** FOL 28";
— Expédier le tout à "**Centre de Voile Valentin**" **44740 BATZ-SUR-MER**;
A réception du bulletin d'inscription, nous vous enverrons un dossier de stage accompagné éventuellement de renseignements complémentaires et conseils utiles pour le séjour.
IMPORTANT : vous munir, avant le stage, d'un certificat médical de non contre-indication à la pratique de la voile, d'une aptitude à la natation et d'une autorisation parentale.
REMBOURSEMENT : Les désistements tardifs portent préjudice à la collectivité, les arrhes sont conservées.

✂

BULLETIN D'INSCRIPTION

NOM _____ Prénom _____

Adresse _____ Date de Naissance _____

m'inscrit au(x) stage(s) :

du _____ au _____ Code _____	Horaire souhaité _____
du _____ au _____ Code _____	Horaire souhaité _____
du _____ au _____ Code _____	Horaire souhaité _____

et verse _____ du _____ au _____ d'arrhes.

SIGNATURE,

"Camp de Jeunes" information and registration form from *Valentin: Ecole de voile*. Reprinted by permission of *Ecole Française de voile*.

PARC DE LA
JACQUES-CARTIER

Les beaux gestes du randonneur

Respectons les règlements du parc...

— Abstenez-vous de jeter des déchets ailleurs que dans les contenants et les endroits prévus à cette fin;

— Veuillez vous conformer à la vocation de chaque sentier : ne pas circuler à vélo sur les sentiers réservés à la randonnée pédestre uniquement;

— S'il vous plaît, demeurez sur les sentiers aménagés et signalés.

Ainsi, tout en profitant de votre randonnée, vous contribuez à conserver les beautés de la nature et à respecter les animaux sauvages. De plus, vous évitez d'endommager les équipements tout en assurant votre propre sécurité.

Collaborons à l'amélioration des sentiers...

— Rangeons sur le côté les bois morts représentant un obstacle sur les sentiers tout en prenant soin de ne pas abîmer les arbres et les plantes du sous-bois;

— Favorisons l'écoulement naturel des eaux en nettoyant les canaux qui permettent l'évacuation des eaux hors du sentier;

— Écartons du sentier les cailloux instables avec le pied, car ils sont parfois cause d'incidents pour le randonneur.

Informez le personnel du parc de tout bris important constaté dans les sentiers

Tous ces gestes que vous pouvez poser prolongeront l'implication de centaines de bénévoles qui participent annuellement au programme d'entretien de sentiers.

Pour de plus amples informations, adressez-vous au personnel à l'accueil.

Vous appréciez la découverte en forêt?

Le réseau de sentiers du parc de la Jacques-Cartier désire s'améliorer avec l'aide des fervents de plein air. Lors de vos randonnées, quelques gestes fort simples permettront de prolonger la durée de vie des sentiers du parc et rendront vos randonnées plus agréables et sécuritaires.

LA PROTECTION DU PARC DE LA JACQUES-CARTIER C'EST...

Sensibiliser ses amis...

...Laisser les animaux se nourrir d'eux-mêmes...

... Laisser les beautés naturelles dans leur décor...

— rapporter tout déchet, à la fin de votre séjour;
— éviter de nourrir les animaux;
— cueillir seulement les fruits comestibles;
— laisser vos animaux domestiques à la maison
— avertir le personnel du parc de tout événement spécial : observation de phénomènes naturels à protéger, bris d'équipements, etc.;

— pratiquer vos activités aux endroits aménagés à cette fin;
— enregistrer vos captures, si vous pratiquez la pêche;
— bien surveiller les annonces du petit lynx;

«Et n'oubliez pas que seuls les castors peuvent couper des arbres dans le parc!»

Éthique

Vous pouvez collaborer à la conservation et au maintien de l'aspect naturel du parc de la Jacques-Cartier. Il vous suffit de :

"Les beaux gestes du randonneur" and "Ethique" from *Parc de la Jacques-Cartier; Fenêtre sur la nature québécoise.* Reprinted by permission of *Société Gestion Activités Commerciales Parc de la Jacques-Cartier.*

❋ Realia 12-3

NIAGARA... TORONTO... OTTAWA... MONTREAL... QUEBEC...

VOYAGE PUBLICITAIRE DE 8 JOURS
VOTRE PROGRAMME

1er jour :
FRANCE - TORONTO - NIAGARA
Départ de votre région en autocar jusqu'à l'aéroport. Assistance aux formalités d'embar-
quement par nos soins. Envol pour le *Canada.* Un *repas* et une *collation* vous seront offerts à bord ainsi
que des boissons. Vous aurez la possibilité de visionner un film, et à votre disposition, des canaux de musiques variées. Accueil à l'arrivée par votre guide-accompagnateur, et départ pour *Niagara Falls.* Dîner libre. Nuit à l'hôtel.

2ème jour :
NIAGARA - TORONTO - MILLE ILES
Après le petit déjeuner, tour d'orientation du site des Chutes du Niagara. Embarquement sur le "Maid of the Mist", robuste petit bateau qui vous emmènera devant les chutes en remontant la rivière jusqu'au cœur du "fer à cheval" formé par celles-ci. Là, vous appréhenderez la force phénoménale et le bruit assourdissant de ces tonnes d'eau qui tombent d'une hauteur de 56 mètres dans la *rivière Niagara.* Déjeuner sur le site. Départ vers *Toronto* en passant par Niagara-on-the-Lake. Dès votre arrivée, tour d'orientation du centre des affaires du Canada : Bay Street, l'Hôtel de Ville, le Parlement, l'Université de Toronto, la Rue Yonge, le Stade Skydome et la tour du CN (la plus haute structure autoportante du monde, 553 mètres de haut, dont l'observatoire culmine à 350 mètres). Continuation vers la région de Mille Iles. *(Croisière des Mille Iles)* Croisière d'une heure dans ce site enchanteur de granit rose et de calcaire - Dîner et logement à l'hôtel.

3ème jour :
MILLE ILES - OTTAWA - COMTE DE PORTNEUF
Après le petit déjeuner, départ vers *Ottawa.* A l'arrivée, un tour d'orientation d'Ottawa, capitale pleine d'espaces verts et d'harmonie : le Parlement, le Musée des Beaux-Arts, le Musée Canadien de la Civilisation, le quartier des ambassades à Rockliffe, le Marché By, le Canal Rideau, la basse ville, la promenade Sussex, le Mille Historique. Déjeuner dans la ville. Continuation vers le *Comté de Portneuf.* A l'arrivée vous serez *accueillis par vos cousins québécois dans leurs demeures.* Après le *dîner traditionnel en famille,* tout le monde se retrouve à la salle communautaire pour la soirée villageoise, où vous chanterez et danserez accompagnés de musiciens et du "caller". Nuit en famille.

4ème jour :
COMTE DE PORTNEUF - QUEBEC
Après un copieux petit déjeuner en famille, départ pour Québec, "la vieille capitale", dominée par ses remparts. Visite des *Chutes de Sainte-Anne.* Découverte de *l'île d'Orléans.* Vous aurez un succulent *déjeuner typique avec musicien* dans une "cabane à sucre" québécoise. Visite de la *Chute de Montmorency.* En fin d'après-midi, arrivée à l'hôtel, installation. Dîner, soirée à thème.

5ème jour :
QUEBEC - MONTREAL
Après le petit déjeuner, *visite guidée de Québec.* Les Plaines d'Abraham, le Parlement, le Château Frontenac, la Place Royale, la Place d'Armes et le Vieux Québec, classé patrimoine mondial par l'UNESCO. Déjeuner dans le Vieux Québec. Temps libre pour la découverte personnelle de la ville. Continuation vers *Montréal.* Installation à l'hôtel. Dîner. Après le repas, nous vous proposons une

sortie *Montréal by night,* retour à l'hôtel et nuit.

6ème jour :
MONTREAL
Petit déjeuner. Ensuite vous serez convié à une démonstration d'articles de marque que vous aurez la possibilité d'acquérir à
des prix très intéressants (sans obliga-tion d'achat). Un verre de l'amitié vous sera offert.
Déjeuner. Après-midi *tour de ville guidé de Montréal* qui vous permettra de découvrir le berceau de la cité fondée en 1642 et appelée *Ville Marie* par le Sieur Chomedey de Maisonneuve sur le site que *Jacques Cartier* baptisa *Mont Réal.* Le Vieux Montréal est un bijou architectural des plus remarquables en Amérique du Nord. La Cathédrale Notre-Dame, l'Oratoire Saint-Joseph, le Quartier "branché" Saint-Laurent, la Rue Saint-Denis, la Rue Sainte Catherine, l'île Sainte-Hélène et son parc d'attraction; l'île Notre-Dame et son célèbre circuit automobile Gilles Villeneuve. *Dîner d'adieu (Homard)* dans une *boîte à chanson* dans le vieux Montréal. Nuit à l'hôtel.

7ème jour :
MONTREAL - FRANCE
Après le petit déjeuner, temps libre pour le shopping et la découverte de la ville souter-raine, gigantesque galerie commerciale jumelée au métro. Déjeuner. En fin d'après-midi, transfert à l'aéroport de Mirabel. Assistance aux formalités d'enre-gistrement. Au cours du vol, un dîner et des boissons vous seront servis.

8ème jour :
FRANCE
Petit déjeuner à bord. Arrivée en France dans la matinée. Débar-quement, prise en charge par
notre autocariste qui vous ramènera dans vos foyers.

N.B. :
Pour des raisons techniques, le circuit pourrait se faire en sens inverse. Formalité : Passeport en cours de validité obligatoire.

From *Canada, pays grandiose: Voyage chez nos cousins d'Amérique.* Reprinted by permission of **Ruban Bleu Voyages.**

R E A L I A

Using Realia 12-1: Camps and registration form

1. **Reading:** As a pre-reading activity, have students list in French any activities they might do at a summer camp. Distribute the realia. Have students make a chart of the different activities available at these camps.

2. **Listening:** Distribute the registration form and allow students time to scan the text. Then describe your stay at one of these camps last summer. Without revealing the name of the camp, tell when you went, how much you paid, what you did, and so on. Students should decide which camp you attended.

3. **Speaking:** Have partners create a conversation between a camp administrator and a student who is interested in attending the camp. The conversation should focus on the activities available, the type of lodging, the dates, prices, and directions to the camp.

4. **Writing:** Have students create a brochure for a real or imaginary summer camp of their choice. Remind students to include several different plans, detailed descriptions and prices, a map showing where the camp is located, and a registration form.

5. **Culture:** Have students tell in what region of France the camps advertised are located. Have them locate the cities of Croisic and Batz-sur-Mer on a map of France. You might have students research on the Internet any similar camps that are located in French-speaking Canada.

Using Realia 12-2: Park rules for Parc de la Jacques-Cartier

1. **Listening:** Distribute copies of the park rules and allow students time to scan the text. Then read aloud several commands concerning behavior in the park area. Have students respond **oui** or **non** according to what the park rules instruct them to do and not do. (**Respectez la nature. (oui) Mutilez les arbres. (non)**)

2. **Reading:** Have students read the park rules and underline the phrases that correspond to the functions in this **étape.** For example, **demeurez sur les sentiers aménagés et signalés** (from the park rules) corresponds to the function **suivre les sentiers balisés** (from the textbook). Students may find several ways to convey the same idea. You might have students share their findings with the class to check their answers and to exchange information.

3. **Speaking:** Have students work in groups to act out a skit. One student plays the role of a park ranger who is leading a group of tourists through a path in the park. As he or she is showing tourists different sights, the tourists keep doing things they shouldn't do. The park ranger has to remind them of the various rules of the park.

4. **Writing:** Have students write a short letter to the park personnel reporting some incidents they saw, while they were hiking in the park, that were against the park rules.

5. **Culture:** Have students locate the Parc de la Jacques-Cartier on a map of Quebec. Then have students locate other parks in the Quebec region. You might bring in information on a local state park or a national park and have students compare the information.

■ **Using Realia: Chapter 12**

Using Realia 12-3: Canadian tour

1. **Reading:** As a pre-reading activity, have students list Canadian cities they know and group them geographically. Then distribute the tour description. Have students create a chart showing the events for each day: what sights are going to be visited, where dinner is being served, how tourists will travel to the next destination, in what city they will be spending the night, and so on.

2. **Listening:** Tell students that you took this tour last year. Describe what you did and saw. Have students trace your itinerary by writing the names of the cities. **D'abord, on a visité le stade Skydome (Toronto); Ensuite, on a vu les plaines d'Abraham (Québec); Après ça, on a fait un tour sur le bateau "Maid of the Mist" (Niagara); On est allés à la Cathédrale Notre-Dame (Montréal); Finalement, on a vu les chutes de Sainte-Anne (Québec).**

3. **Speaking:** Have partners act out a conversation between two people who took this tour. One enjoyed it thoroughly and the other was disappointed.

4. **Writing:** Have students create a brochure for a vacation package to France for Canadians. They should model their brochure on the tour description, but substitute sights and activities in French cities and regions.

5. **Culture:** Point out to students that one of the sights visited on the tour is the location that Jacques Cartier originally named *Mont Réal.* Have students research how Montreal got its name and the important events surrounding the history of the city.

REALIA

Situation Cards

Situation 1-1: Interview

Imagine that I'm the coordinator of a student exchange program. I'm going to ask you a few questions to help me place you with a French family.

Tu as quel âge?

Tu es comment? Timide? Sympa?

Qu'est-ce que tu aimes faire après l'école?

Qu'est-ce que tu aimes comme sports?

Quel est ton cours préféré? Pourquoi?

Situation 1-2: Interview

Imagine that I'm your French pen pal. I'm going to be an exchange student at your school next year. I'd like your advice on what to pack.

Qu'est-ce qu'on met pour aller à l'école?

Et pour sortir, qu'est-ce qu'on met?

A ton avis, est-ce que je prends un maillot de bain? Un anorak? Un imperméable?

Qu'est-ce que je dois prendre d'autre?

Qu'est-ce que je peux acheter comme cadeau pour ta famille?

Situation 1-3: Interview

You don't know what to do this weekend. I'm going to make some suggestions. Tell me what you think of them.

Pourquoi tu n'invites pas des amis chez toi vendredi soir?

Tu as envie de faire les magasins samedi après-midi?

Ça te dit de manger dans un restaurant samedi soir?

On pourrait aller à un match de foot vendredi soir. Ça te dit?

Pourquoi tu n'étudies pas tout le week-end?

SITUATION CARDS

Situation Cards 1-1, 1-2, 1-3: Role-plays

Situation 1-1: Role-play

Student A   Imagine that you're one of your favorite TV or movie stars. Your partner will try to guess who you are. Answer all of your partner's questions, but don't volunteer any extra information.

Student B   Your partner is pretending to be one of his or her favorite TV or movie stars. Try to guess who he or she is by asking questions about his or her age, height, hair color, personality, and interests.

Situation 1-2: Role-play

Student A   Your partner plans to climb Mont Blanc in France (elevation 15,771 feet). He or she has only packed some shorts, T-shirts, and tennis shoes. Suggest more appropriate clothing and other items your partner should bring.

Student B   You've decided to climb Mont Blanc in France (elevation 15,771 feet). You've packed some shorts, T-shirts, and tennis shoes. Your partner will suggest other items you should take. Resist his or her suggestions: you like to travel lightly!

Situation 1-3: Role-play

Student A   Imagine that you and your partner have a French test tomorrow. You know that you should be studying for the test, but you'd rather have some fun instead. Try to get your partner to join you by suggesting things you could do together.

Student B   Imagine that you and your partner have a French test tomorrow. You're very conscientious and plan to study for the test. Your partner wants to have fun instead and suggests other activities. Resist all of his or her suggestions and make some of your own.

SITUATION CARDS

Situation 2-1: Interview

You're an exchange student in France, and I'm the parent of your French host. I'll welcome you to our home. Respond appropriately.

Bienvenue chez nous! Fais comme chez toi.

Tu as fait bon voyage?

Ça va? Pas trop fatigué(e)?

Tu n'as pas faim?

Est-ce que tu as soif?

Situation 2-2: Interview

Imagine that you're building a house and that you have unlimited funds. Make a sketch of the floor plan. I'll ask you where things are.

Elle est où, la cuisine?

Où est ta chambre?

Qu'est-ce qu'il y a dans ta chambre?

Où est le salon?

Qu'est-ce qu'il y a dans le salon?

Situation 2-3: Interview

I'm a French student, and I've just arrived at your school. I'd like to learn my way around town, so I'll ask you how to get to several places.

Je cherche la bibliothèque, s'il te plaît.

Où est la poste, s'il te plaît?

Est-ce qu'il y a une piscine près d'ici?

Je cherche un fast-food, s'il te plaît.

Il y a un parc près d'ici?

S I T U A T I O N   C A R D S

Situation Cards 2-1, 2-2, 2-3: Role-plays

Situation 2-1: Role-play

Student A   You're hosting an exchange student who'll be spending a week with your family. When the student arrives, he or she is exhausted. Welcome your guest and try to make him or her feel at home. Offer something to eat and drink, too.

Student A   You're taking part in an exchange program. You've just arrived at your host's home after hours of travel and a lot of problems. You haven't eaten in a long time, and you're exhausted. Respond to your host's welcome politely, but truthfully.

Situation 2-2: Role-play

Student A   Your family has just moved into a new home. You're showing your best friend your room. Point out several items and respond to any compliments your friend makes.

Student B   Your best friend has just moved into a new home. Your friend is showing you his or her room. Make several complimentary remarks about things you see.

Situation 2-3: Role-play

Student A   Using the map of Chartres on page 46 of your textbook, direct a tourist from the train station to the cathedral. If the tourist seems confused, be sure to repeat the directions more clearly.

Student B   Look at the map of Chartres on page 46 of your textbook. You're a tourist in Chartres, trying to get from the train station to the cathedral. Ask your partner, who lives in Chartres, to direct you. You start to repeat the directions after your partner, but you get confused and ask your partner to repeat the directions.

French 2 Allez, viens!, Chapter 2

SITUATION CARDS

Situation 3-1: Interview

You're an exchange student in France. You offer to do the grocery shopping for your host family. I'll be the salesperson at each of the small shops you go to. At each store, first ask the price of one food item. Then ask for enough of that item to feed six people. Finally, ask for the total cost of your purchase.

(à la boulangerie) **Qu'est-ce que vous désirez?**

(à la crémerie) **Vous désirez?**

(à la boucherie) **Qu'est-ce que vous désirez?**

(à la poissonnerie) **Vous désirez?**

(à la pâtisserie) **Qu'est-ce que vous désirez?**

Situation 3-2: Interview

Imagine that you're having dinner at the home of your French host family. I'm your host. We're having chicken, potatoes, and peas.

Tu veux encore du poulet?

Je te donne des pommes de terre?

Et comme légumes, j'ai préparé des petits pois. Tu en veux?

(Ask me to pass you something.)

(Compliment me on the meal.)

Situation 3-3: Interview

I don't know what to give my mother for her birthday. I need your advice.

Qu'est-ce que je peux offrir à ma mère?

Je pense lui offrir un sac à main. Qu'en penses-tu?

L'inviter au restaurant, c'est une bonne idée?

Elle est très sportive. Tu as une idée de cadeau?

Une plante verte, c'est une bonne idée ou c'est trop banal?

Situation Cards 3-1, 3-2, 3-3: Role-plays

Situation 3-1: Role-play

Student A   You're the salesperson at a small grocery store in France. It's five minutes before closing time, and you're tired and ready to go home. A customer walks in with a very long shopping list. Answer all of his or her questions about prices.

Student B   You walk into a small grocery store in France five minutes before closing time. You have a very long shopping list and an extremely tight budget. Ask how much each item on your list costs. Then ask for a specific quantity. Ask for the total of your purchases.

Situation 3-2: Role-play

Student A   Your friend has invited you over for an escargot pizza! At first, you avoid trying the pizza by asking for salad, bread, and more water. Your friend insists that you try a slice. Accept or refuse another slice of the pizza.

Student B   You've invited a friend over to share an escargot pizza with you, but he or she is reluctant to try it. Pass your friend the other items that he or she requests, but keep offering the pizza until he or she takes a slice. Then offer another slice.

Situation 3-3: Role-play

Student A   You're trying to decide on a birthday present for your best friend. Ask your partner for suggestions. Reject the first few suggestions and explain why they aren't acceptable. Finally, accept one of the suggestions and tell why it's the perfect gift idea.

Student B   Your partner asks you for advice on a birthday present for his or her best friend. He or she rejects the first few suggestions you make. Keep coming up with gift ideas until your partner accepts one of your suggestions.

Situation 4-1: Interview

I'd like to know more about your favorite city. Ask me about my favorite city, too.

Quelle est ta ville préférée?

Où est-ce qu'elle se trouve?

C'est comment?

Qu'est-ce qu'il y a à voir là-bas? Et à faire?

(Ask me about my favorite city.)

Situation 4-2: Interview

I'm going to tell you some of my likes and dislikes and then ask you about your likes and dislikes.

Ce que je n'aime pas manger, c'est _____. Et toi?

Ce qui m'ennuie à l'école, c'est (de) _____. Et toi?

Ce qui me plaît le week-end, c'est (de) _____. Et toi?

Ce que je préfère comme sport, c'est _____. Et toi?

Ce que j'aime bien faire avec mes amis, c'est _____. Et toi?

Situation 4-3: Interview

Let's talk about what you do on a typical Saturday.

A quelle heure est-ce que tu te lèves?

Qu'est-ce que tu fais pour te préparer le matin?

Qu'est-ce que tu aimes faire l'après-midi? Et le soir?

A quelle heure est-ce que tu te couches?

SITUATION CARDS

Situation Cards 4-1, 4-2, 4-3: Role-plays

Situation 4-1: Role-play

Student A You've won a two-week vacation anywhere in the world. Your travel agent suggests Martinique. Ask him or her about Martinique, where it's located, what it's like, what the weather is like, and what there is to see and do there.

Student B You're a travel agent. A customer asks you to suggest a good vacation destination. Suggest that he or she go to Martinique. Answer the customer's questions about Martinique.

Situation 4-2: Role-play

Student A You live in Martinique. Your pen pal from the United States is coming to spend two weeks with you. Find out a few things your pen pal likes to do. Then suggest some activities the two of you could do together.

Student B You're visiting your pen pal in Martinique. Your friend wants to know what you like to do. Ask about his or her likes and dislikes, too. Accept or reject your friend's suggestions politely.

Situation 4-3: Role-play

Student A You're a scientist. You've designed a robot to take your place at home and at school while you're away on a trip to Martinique. Program your robot by telling it your daily routine. Repeat any details your robot misses when it short circuits.

Student B You're a robot being programmed to follow the daily routine of the scientist who created you. Repeat the daily routine after the scientist. You are prone to short circuit and must "re-enter" some of the steps.

SITUATION CARDS

French 2 Allez, viens!, Chapter 4

Situation 5-1: Interview

You don't look well. I'll ask you what's wrong. Tell me about the terrible day you've had.

Ça n'a pas l'air d'aller. Qu'est-ce qui se passe?

Allez, raconte! Qu'est-ce qui t'arrive?

Situation 5-2: Interview

Yesterday was the first day of school after a long vacation. I was absent, and you had a substitute teacher. I'm going to ask you how your vacation was and how your first day back from vacation was. Ask me about my vacation.

Comment se sont passées tes vacances?

Qu'est-ce que tu as fait?

Ça s'est bien passé, hier?

Comment ça s'est passé avec l'autre prof?

Situation 5-3: Interview

I'm going to mention some school subjects. Tell me how you do in each one.

En maths?

En sciences naturelles?

En sport?

En anglais?

En français?

En histoire?

SITUATION CARDS

Situation Cards 5-1, 5-2, 5-3: Role-plays

Situation 5-1: Role-play

Student A You've had a really bad day. Phone your friend and tell him or her everything that went wrong today. Your friend sympathizes with you and consoles you, but you can tell that something is wrong. Ask your friend what happened.

Student B Your friend calls to tell you about his or her bad day. You sympathize with and console your friend even though you've had a bad day yourself. When your friend expresses concern, tell what happened.

Situation 5-2: Role-play

Student A You and your friend are catching up after a long vacation. Your vacation was fantastic, except for this past weekend when everything went wrong. Tell about your fantastic vacation and your disastrous weekend. Ask about your partner's vacation.

Student B You and your friend are catching up after a long vacation. Your vacation was a disaster. Everything went wrong up until this past weekend. Tell about your disastrous vacation and your terrific weekend. Ask about your partner's vacation.

Situation 5-3: Role-play

Student A Your son or daughter arrives home late from school after serving detention for goofing off in class. First, scold your son or daughter. Then ask about his or her grades in several classes. Congratulate him or her on any good grades and ask for an explanation of any bad grades.

Student B You've just finished serving detention for goofing off in class. Your parent will scold you and then ask about your grades in several classes. Tell him or her your grades. Make excuses for any bad grades you received.

SITUATION CARDS

Situation Cards 6-1, 6-2, 6-3: Interviews

Situation 6-1: Interview

I'm going to ask you about amusement parks and zoos that you've visited.

Est-ce que tu as visité un parc d'attractions récemment? Lequel?

Tu t'es bien amusé(e)? Qu'est-ce que tu as fait?

Est-ce que tu aimes aller au zoo? Lesquels as-tu visités?

Et _(name of zoo),_ **c'était comment? Ça t'a plu?**

(Ask me if I've visited an amusement park or zoo and how I liked it.)

Situation 6-2: Interview

I'm going to tell you some unusual things about our school. React to them with disbelief.

Tu sais que notre directeur chante dans un groupe de rock?

Il y a un million de dollars caché dans un livre à la bibliothèque.

La cantine de notre école a gagné le premier prix du Cordon Bleu!

Il y a une tour romane au-dessus du gymnase.

Situation 6-3: Interview

Imagine that you're an exchange student in Tours. You're doing a report for school on Leonardo da Vinci, so you decide to take a tour of the Louvre and see the Mona Lisa. I'm the ticket agent you talk to about getting your ticket to Paris.

(Ask me when the train for Paris leaves and from which platform.)

(Ask me how much a round-trip ticket costs and ask for one ticket.)

(Ask me if I know when the Louvre opens and when it closes.)

(Ask me if I know how much the entrance fee is.)

SITUATION CARDS

Situation Cards 6-1, 6-2, 6-3: Role-plays

Situation 6-1: Role-play

Student A   You missed a chance to spend a week in France with your friends because your family had already planned a vacation at an amusement park. Ask your friend about his or her trip to France. Tell about your trip.

Student B   You just got back from a week in France. Your partner couldn't go because of a family trip to an amusement park. Tell him or her about the castles you visited and the fun you had in France. Ask him or her how the amusement park was.

Situation 6-2: Role-play

Student A   You arrive in class without your homework. Make up a fantastic excuse for not having it. The teacher reacts with disbelief, so you try another excuse. The teacher still doesn't believe you, so you tell the real reason.

Student B   You're a teacher. A student who doesn't have his or her homework gives you two outrageous excuses, and you react to them with disbelief. Finally, the student tells you the real reason. You react appropriately.

Situation 6-3: Role-play

Student A   Last weekend, your travel agent persuaded you to go on a sight-seeing tour. You had a terrible time. Tell the agent what you thought of the tour. The agent tells you about another tour. Make travel arrangements.

Student B   You're a travel agent. A customer is complaining about a tour you recommended. You took the same tour recently and you react with disbelief. Describe another tour that you enjoyed. Help your customer make travel arrangements.

Situation 7-1: Interview

We're going to ask each other how we feel and point out all of our aches and pains. If you don't actually have any, make up a few.

Tu n'as pas l'air en forme. Qu'est-ce que tu as?

Tu as l'air tout(e) raplapla. Qu'est-ce qui t'arrive?

Tu as mal où?

Moi, j'ai mal partout!

(Ask me what's wrong.)

Situation 7-2: Interview

We're going to give each other advice and encouragement on keeping fit.

Tu fais du sport? Pourquoi ou pourquoi pas?

Tu ferais bien de faire/jouer *(name of a sport).*

Pourquoi tu ne fais pas cent abdominaux chaque jour pour te mettre en forme?

Je suis tout(e) raplapla. Qu'est-ce que tu me conseilles?

Je n'ai pas très envie de faire de l'exercice.

Situation 7-3: Interview

We're going to talk about our personal health habits.

Est-ce que tu manges des légumes? Pourquoi ou pourquoi pas?

Qu'est-ce que tu évites de faire pour rester en forme?

Qu'est-ce qu'on doit manger ou ne pas manger pour rester en forme?

Moi, je me couche très tard.

Je déjeune toujours au fast-food.

SITUATION CARDS

Situation Cards 7-1, 7-2, 7-3: Role-plays

Situation 7-1: Role-play

Student A You're the school nurse. You're used to dealing with students who aren't really sick. When a student comes in, find out what the problem is. If you think the student is faking an illness, send the student back to class.

Student B You forgot to study for a math test! You make up a complaint and go to the school nurse, hoping to be sent home for the day. This nurse has seen a lot of students who weren't really sick, so you will have to be very convincing.

Situation 7-2: Role-play

Student A You're not very enthusiastic about exercise. You've been teamed up in gym class with someone who loves to work out. Your partner gives you advice on how to get into shape. At first, you react negatively. You finally agree to do some sit-ups, push-ups, or weight-lifting. You express discouragement as you exercise.

Student B You're really "into" physical fitness. You've been teamed up in gym class with someone who doesn't like to work out. Make suggestions about training and sports. Try to get your partner to do some exercises. Offer encouragement.

Situation 7-3: Role-play

Student A You're watching TV with a friend. He or she is munching on unhealthy snacks. Comment on the snacks and make some suggestions about eating healthier foods. Be prepared to justify your suggestions.

Student B You're watching TV and eating snacks with a friend. He or she makes some remarks about the snacks and suggests healthier foods. Reject all of his or her suggestions and ask why you have to eat all this healthy food.

SITUATION CARDS

French 2 Allez, viens!, Chapter 7

Situation 8-1: Interview

Imagine you've moved here from another town. I'll ask you about your former school and friends and about the place you used to live.

A quelle école est-ce que tu allais avant?

Est-ce que ton école te manque? Pourquoi?

Est-ce que tu peux décrire un prof qui te manque?

Est-ce que tu as un ami ou une amie qui te manque?

Est-ce qu'il y a une ville qui te manque? C'était comment?

Situation 8-2: Interview

I'm going to ask you some questions about your childhood. You can make up stories if you wish.

Quand tu étais petit(e), qu'est-ce que tu aimais faire?

L'école, c'était comment quand tu avais six ans? Et maintenant?

Est-ce que tu avais des responsabilités? Lesquelles?

Quand tu étais petit(e), quel était ton rêve?

Quand tu avais douze ans, tu étais comment? Et maintenant?

Situation 8-3: Interview

Imagine that we're planning a field trip. I'll suggest some places we could go. Tell me what you think of my suggestions. Then I'll ask you to suggest a few places.

Si on mangeait dans un restaurant français?

Si on visitait un musée?

Si on allait en Côte d'Ivoire?

Si on allait à un concert de musique classique?

Qu'est-ce que tu proposes?

Situation Cards 8-1, 8-2, 8-3: Role-plays

Situation 8-1: Role-play

Student A   You've moved and you're going to a new school. Phone your best friend from your former town or neighborhood and tell him or her what you miss. It could be your school, your friends, the things you used to do, or the places you used to go.

Student B   You're talking on the phone to your best friend who has recently moved away. Your friend misses your town or neighborhood. Be reassuring and help your friend make the best of it.

Situation 8-2: Role-play

Student A   You're a grandparent talking with your grandchild. Answer your grandchild's questions about life when you were a teenager. You believe that today's conveniences make life easier than when you were a teenager.

Student B   Ask your grandfather or grandmother about life when he or she was a teenager. Ask him or her questions about what he or she was like, what he or she used to do for fun, and how things were different.

Situation 8-3: Role-play

Student A   You're visiting Abidjan with your partner. You're very excited to be in Abidjan, but your partner is homesick. Reassure your partner and then suggest some activities you could do together. Keep making suggestions until your partner finally agrees to one.

Student B   You're visiting Abidjan with your partner. Your partner is excited to be in Abidjan, but you're homesick and don't feel like doing anything. Reject the activities he or she suggests and tell what you miss back home. Finally, agree to one of his or her suggestions.

SITUATION CARDS

Situation 9-1: Interview

I'm going to suggest some possibilities to you. Accept or reject the possibilities.

A mon avis, il va pleuvoir aujourd'hui.

Je parie que tu vas aller en France un jour.

Tu es de bonne humeur aujourd'hui. Peut-être que tu es amoureux (amoureuse)!

Je crois que nous avons une interro de français cette semaine.

Tu as l'air déprimé(e). Peut-être que tu as beaucoup de devoirs à faire ce week-end.

Situation 9-2: Interview

I'll start to tell you some news I know. Show interest in what I'm about to tell you. Then I'll ask you to tell me some news.

Tu connais la nouvelle?

Devine ce que j'ai fait!

(Tell me some school news.)

(Tell me about something that happened outside of school.)

Situation 9-3: Interview

Imagine you've been "grounded." Answer my questions.

Qu'est-ce qui s'est passé?

Alors, qu'est-ce que tu as fait?

A ce moment-là, tes parents, ils avaient l'air fâchés?

Bref, comment ça s'est terminé?

Situation Cards 9-1, 9-2, 9-3: Role-plays

Situation 9-1: Role-play

Student A You're a French director auditioning an actor. Test this person's acting ability by telling him or her to look surprised, worried, angry, in love, and so on. The actor asks for more information. Explain why he or she might be experiencing the emotions.

Student B You're an actor/actress auditioning for a role. When the director asks you to act out an emotion, ask him or her *why* you are feeling that way, so that you can perform better. Accept or reject the director's explanations.

Situation 9-2: Role-play

Student A You and your boyfriend or girlfriend broke up last month, but you're still interested in him or her. Your friend has heard some gossip about your ex. At first, you pretend not to be interested, but you finally show interest in what your friend has to say.

Student B You've heard some gossip about your friend's ex-boyfriend or girlfriend. You know that your friend is still interested in that person, so you're eager to tell your friend the latest news about his or her ex.

Situation 9-3: Role-play

Student A You're in detention for the tenth time this year. You're surprised to see your friend there. You can't resist trying to guess why your friend got the detention. Your guess is wrong, and your friend tells you the story. Tell your friend why you're in detention.

Student B You and your friend are in detention. This is the first time you've ever had detention. Your friend tries to guess why you got the detention. You tell your friend the story.

SITUATION CARDS

Situation 10-1: Interview

I'm going to ask you to help me with a personal problem I have.
Je peux te parler?
Je me suis disputé(e) avec un(e) ami(e).
A ton avis, qu'est-ce que je dois faire?
Et toi, ça n'a pas l'air d'aller. Qu'est-ce qui se passe?

Situation 10-2: Interview

I'm going to ask you to do me some favors. Agree to some and make excuses for others.
Dis, tu peux m'aider? Tu pourrais rendre ce livre à la bibliothèque?
Ça t'ennuie de me prêter dix dollars?
Ça t'embête de préparer des amuse-gueule pour ma boum?
(Ask me a small favor.)
(Ask me an unreasonable favor.)

Situation 10-3: Interview

I've done some things I need to apologize for. You can either accept my apologies or reproach me.
Je n'aurais pas dû lire la lettre de ton petit ami (ta petite amie) à la classe. Tu ne m'en veux pas?
Et j'ai lu ton journal, aussi. Excuse-moi.
Dis, tu ne m'en veux pas d'avoir mangé ton déjeuner?
(Apologize for something you've done recently.)

SITUATION CARDS

Situation Cards 10-1, 10-2, 10-3: Role-plays

Situation 10-1: Role-play

Student A   You've just had a misunderstanding with your best friend who thinks you still owe him or her ten dollars. You think you've paid the money back. Discuss this problem with your partner and ask for advice.

Student B   Listen as your friend tells you about a misunderstanding he or she had with a friend. Ask for explanations until you have the full story. Tell your partner what you think he or she should do.

Situation 10-2: Role-play

Student A   You're friends with all your classmates. Your partner will ask you several favors. Agree to some of them, but if your friend tries to take advantage of your good will, feel free to turn him or her down.

Student B   Your partner is a good friend who does favors for everyone. You're having a party and you need several favors. Ask your partner to do as many favors as he or she will agree to.

Situation 10-3: Role-play

Student A   You lost your partner's favorite CD. You can see he or she is really angry. Tell him or her how sorry you are. It won't be easy to get your apology accepted.

Student B   You've just found out that your partner lost your favorite CD. You're really angry. Tell your partner how you feel, but finally accept his or her apology.

SITUATION CARDS

Situation 11-1: Interview

I'm going to ask you about your tastes in music.

Qui est ton chanteur (ta chanteuse) préféré(e)?

Quel genre de musique est le plus populaire parmi tes amis?

Tu connais _____?

(Ask me if I know a musician or group. Think of one I probably know.)

(Ask me about another musician or group that I probably don't know.)

Situation 11-2: Interview

I'm going to ask you about some films that are currently playing.

Qu'est-ce qu'on joue comme films d'action? Ça passe où?

On joue un bon film comique en ce moment? C'est avec qui?

Qu'est-ce que tu préfères comme films? Les histoires d'amour? Les films d'action? Les films comiques?

Quel film tu veux voir ce week-end?

(Ask me what kind of film I prefer.)

Situation 11-3: Interview

I'm going to ask you some questions about books.

Quel est ton livre préféré?

C'est quel genre de livre?

De quoi ça parle?

Est-ce que tu lis des livres de poésie? Pourquoi? Pourquoi pas?

Quels livres est-ce que tu lis pour ton cours d'anglais? Ils sont intéressants?

(I'll name some book titles. Tell me what you think of each book.)

SITUATION CARDS

Situation Cards 11-1, 11-2, 11-3: Role-plays

Situation 11-1: Role-play

Student A You're throwing a party on your birthday and you've hired a disc jockey. The DJ is playing music that you and your friends don't like. Ask if he or she knows any of the groups or musicians that you and your friends like to dance to and describe the music they play.

Student B You're a disc jockey at a birthday party. You notice that nobody is dancing. The host asks if you're familiar with several groups and musicians that you've never heard of. Finally, he or she mentions a group you know, and you agree to play their music.

Situation 11-2: Role-play

Student A You and your friend are trying to decide on a movie. You love action, horror, and western movies. Suggest several movies and describe them. Reject your friend's suggestions. Finally, agree on a comedy.

Student B You and your friend are trying to decide on a movie. You like science-fiction, classic, and romantic movies. Suggest several movies and describe them. Reject your friend's suggestions. Finally, agree on a comedy.

Situation 11-3: Role-play

Student A You're browsing in a bookstore. A determined salesperson follows you around, recommending books and telling you about them. At first, you reject the salesperson's suggestions. Finally, you buy a book that interests you.

Student B You're a salesperson in a bookstore. Follow a customer around and recommend and describe several books to him or her. Don't give up until you interest the customer in a book.

SITUATION CARDS

Situation 12-1: Interview

I'm going to ask you about your experiences with outdoor activities. If you can't think of any, you can make some up.

Tu as déjà fait du camping?

Où se trouve le parc où tu es allé(e)?

Avec qui est-ce que tu y es allé(e)?

Qu'est-ce qu'il y a à faire là-bas?

Tu as déjà vu des ratons laveurs? Un ours? Des écureuils? Un orignal?

Situation 12-2: Interview

Imagine that we're going camping. You've been camping before, but I haven't. I'll ask some questions and express my concerns.

Qu'est-ce que je dois emporter?

Je voudrais respecter la nature. Qu'est-ce que je dois faire ou ne pas faire?

Est-ce qu'il y a des ours là-bas?

J'ai peur des serpents!

Situation 12-3: Interview

Tell me about the best (or worst) camping, biking, or hiking trip you ever went on. If you've never done any of these activities, make up a story.

Tu es allé(e) où?

Qu'est-ce qu'il y avait à faire?

Qu'est-ce que tu as fait d'abord?

Et ensuite? Après ça?

Comment c'était?

SITUATION CARDS

Situation Cards 12-1, 12-2, 12-3: Role-plays

Situation 12-1: Role-play

Student A Convince your partner to go on a camping trip with you. Tell your partner about the things you can do while camping. Your partner has never gone camping and is very fearful of the animals you might meet. Reassure your partner.

Student B Your partner is trying to get you to go on your first camping trip. Ask questions about the trip. You're very fearful of the animals you might meet. Share your concerns with your partner.

Situation 12-2: Role-play

Student A You're camping with a friend who does nothing but complain. At first you try to encourage your friend. You then discover that he or she forgot to bring some of the camping equipment. Reproach your friend.

Student B You're camping with a friend and you're not enjoying the experience. Complain and express your discouragement. Your friend is sympathetic at first, but then gets angry when he or she finds out you forgot to bring some of the camping equipment. Apologize and try to cheer up your friend.

Situation 12-3: Role-play

Student A You've just come back from a great camping trip with your parent. Tell your friend (your partner) all about the activities you did and how you felt when you were there. Answer his or her questions.

Student B Your friend (your partner) has just come back from a great camping trip with his or her parent. Ask what there was to see and do and what he or she did first, next, and so on.